To Diane,

Thanks for your support
the years. Hopefully my name will
on the next one!

Love,
Kenny
1/3/06

My Life

with the

Hustler

My Life
with the
Hustler

~ JAMIE GRIGGS TEVIS ~

MY LIFE WITH THE HUSTLER

Published by GreatUnpublished.com

For information, please contact:

Jamie Griggs Tevis
15 Ohio Avenue
Athens, Ohio 45701
jamie@frognet.net

Printed in the United States of America

Book Design by Tina Burger

ISBN: 1-58898-908-9

DEDICATION

For my children Will and Julie and for Ryan, Caleb, Adrienne, Ethan, Jonathan and Elizabeth, my children's children.

ACKNOWLEDGEMENTS

I wish to thank the Athens Writers' Group for giving me the courage to begin such a large undertaking and to give special thanks to Dr. James Birchfield of the University of Kentucky Library for his continued support and encouragement through the years.

I must give thanks to many others as well: Kacey Kowars for sharing his research on Walter and his work; Jack Matthews for writing the foreword; Dr. Steven Gwinn and David Sanders for encouraging remarks after reading the manuscript; Jim Fingar for his many hours at the computer, his organizational and editing skills, and his dedication to the project; Betty Craddock, Nancy Roe, T.J. Luce, Arline McCarthy and Tina Burger for their editing assistance; everyone who contributed to the memories of Walter; and to my friend Joe Agranoff for his continuing patience throughout the writing of this book.

Two roads diverged in a wood, and I —
I took the one less traveled by,
And that has made all the difference

"The Road Not Taken"
By Robert Frost

CONTENTS

PREFACE

Walter Tevis was a writer with staying power. He was author of seven novels, twenty-five short stories which appeared in popular magazines, and one television play. His first novel, *The Hustler* (1959), became a hit movie with Paul Newman and Jackie Gleason. The movie was nominated for several Academy Awards. His second novel, *The Man Who Fell to Earth* (1963) with David Bowie, was also made into a movie. The sequel to *The Hustler* was *The Color of Money*, published days before Tevis died in 1984. Paul Newman received an Oscar for his role as Fast Eddie in the movie version of the sequel.

The source of Tevis' inspiration for his books has generated much popular and academic speculation. Several people have even claimed to be characters from his books.

Tevis was born in California February 28, 1928. In 1939 he moved to Lexington, Kentucky.

After a short hitch with the Navy in 1945-46, he attended the University of Kentucky and got a bachelor's degree in English.

Two master's degrees followed, the first in 1955 from the University of Kentucky, and the second in 1961 from the University of Iowa.

He married Jamie Griggs in 1952. They had two children.

Walter Tevis died on August 9, 1984.

FOREWORD

Married for twenty-seven years to the author of *The Hustler*, Jamie Tevis has herself written a most interesting book, one that conveys much about the troubled and agonized writer who invented such legendary figures as Minnesota Fats and Fast Eddie, thereby adding to the folklore of 20th century America. Hers is a book that perfectly suits our contemporary passion for memoirs.

Jack Matthews
July 10, 2001

PART ONE:
I REMEMBER THE HUSTLER

INTRODUCTION TO PART I
WALTER TEVIS VS. THE IMPOSTER, MINNESOTA FATS

"I made up Minnesota Fats–name
and all–as surely as Disney made up
Donald Duck." –Walter Tevis

Walter and I had only been married a few years when he wrote *The Hustler*. That was 1957. Our second child, Julia, was just a baby and we were living in a duplex in Lexington, Kentucky. Walter had completed his MA degree and was working as an editor at the Kentucky Highway Department.

When the book was published in 1959, Walter was teaching at the Covington branch of the University of Kentucky. The success of *The Hustler* changed our lives and opened many doors. The $25,000 he got for it seemed like a lot when Walter's salary was $4,000 a year.

We went to the movie opening of *The Hustler* in New York City in 1961. Walter liked what producer/director Robert Rossen had done with his characters. Jackie Gleason executed the pool shots with great delicacy and grace as Walter had described Minnesota Fats. Walter thought that Paul Newman, the cocky young man, was just right for the part of Fast Eddie.

Impostors began appearing soon after *The Hustler* came out. Through the years several have claimed that they were the real Fast Eddie or the real Minnesota Fats.

The most successful impostor was Rudolf Wanderone. Calling himself Minnesota Fats, he appeared on the Tonight Show telling Johnny Carson and the world that the book and movie were about him. Using the name Walter invented, he endorsed pool tables, cues, and chalk. He made more money on his phony claim than Walter made on both the novel and the movie. He told Johnny Carson, "I have so much money that when a bird flies over my Cadillac, I buy another one rather than wash it."

Of course Walter was annoyed and asked a lawyer about suing. He was told that if someone had wanted to call himself Huckleberry Finn or David Copperfield, Mark Twain or Charles Dickens couldn't have done anything about it. Walter had to live with the impostors and came to consider it a form of flattery that seedy characters knew of his work. Walter told himself that he had entered a place that had not been written about before, and it made some people happy to think that their way of life was worthy of notice. He tried to be philosophical about it, but it still annoyed him.

It bothered him enough that in April 1968 he wrote this letter to Bill Burns, the editor of the now-defunct *Sports-Views* magazine. In that letter he wrote, "Maybe my reason for being upset will be clear. Sometime after the movie came out this man, Rudolf Wanderone, a man whom I had never met, began to capitalize on the fact that he was fat and that he played pool passing well and that *The Hustler* had been pretty successful."

Eventually, to set the record straight, Walter insisted that this author's note be placed in all subsequent editions of *The Hustler*:

> I once saw a fat pool player with a
> facial tic. I once saw another pool
> player who was physically graceful.
> Both were minor hustlers, as far as I
> could tell. Both seemed loud and
> vain–with little dignity and grace,
> unlike my fat pool player. After *The
> Hustler* was published, one of them

claimed to "be" Minnesota Fats.
That is ridiculous. I *made up* Minne-
sota Fats–name and all–as surely as
Disney made up Donald Duck."

It is shameful for con men to make money from other people's work, but after all they are con men. It is more shameful that news organizations have been running stories off and on for years that seem to confirm one impostor's story or another. As recently as March of 2001, the Associated Press picked up the obituary of Eddie Parker (another imposter) after he died in Texas. The AP reported that Parker was the model for the lead character in *The Hustler*, "Fast Eddie." *Time*, *People*, and newspapers all over the country ran this nonsense. Even National Public Radio repeated it. *The Hustler* is still being hustled forty-two years after it was first published.

Fortunately, Walter's work has attracted attention from more than con men and sloppy news organizations. I am still occasionally contacted by literature or film scholars with questions.

For forty years, critics, scholars, and impostors have been claiming to know about Walter Tevis and "the Hustler." Now I want to tell the true story. I know it because I lived with the Hustler for twenty-seven years.

Jamie Tevis

CHAPTER 1
OUR EARLY YEARS TOGETHER
(SEPTEMBER 1952- AUGUST 1960

I Meet the Hustler

I was standing outside the principal's door waiting to be introduced to the small faculty of Carlisle High School in the fall of 1952. A tall, lean, blond fellow, wearing an ill-fitting jacket and frayed pants, pulling on a cigarette and waving it in the air, introduced himself. "My name is Walter Tevis. I'm the new English teacher. Are you nervous?"

"Yes," I answered. "This is my first job. I just graduated from Eastern in the spring, and I have come here to teach home economics."

"There is nothing to be nervous about," he answered me. "This is my third teaching job, so I'm not nervous."

After that I didn't take much serious notice of the single English teacher until one day we were going to a school assembly and he noticed I was wearing a different shade of lipstick. I wasn't accustomed to such close attention. He began coming down to the home economics room in the mornings for a quick cup of instant coffee before his first class.

Carlisle High was a warm, friendly Kentucky school, and we were made to feel at ease by the faculty and students. Being two of the three single people on the faculty in a small town, Walter and I saw a lot of each other. We sold coffee and popcorn at the football games and hung out at the drugstore with the students. No smoking was allowed at the school, so I often strolled with him off school grounds. While he smoked he told me about his family, his experiences in the Navy, and how he was going to become a writer.

One day he sent me a polished red apple to my classroom by way of one of the freshman students we shared. I sent him a note on a small piece of folded paper saying, "Thank you for the big red apple." I drew a picture of the apple with my red marking pencil and sent it to him when the students changed classes. He kept the little note in his billfold for many years, until the paper wore out. That was the beginning of a relationship that lasted for twenty-seven years.

On weekends we often rode the bus to Lexington, where Walter introduced me to his beloved hometown. He took me to meet his Aunt Sallie, who lived on Walton Avenue. Here he had come from California to live with his family as a young boy during the Depression. He took me to the basement to show me what had been his makeshift living quarters during his student days while attending the University of Kentucky on the G.I. Bill. I was not impressed with the hot plate, cot, and temporary shower arrangement. After tuition and books were paid, he had $20 left of the $75 allotment for food, clothes, and spending money. He supplemented his income by working at a poolroom run by his friend from childhood Toby Kavanaugh. Oatmeal cooked on the hot plate was his diet staple when funds ran out.

While in Lexington, we ate at his favorite inexpensive spots: Wings Chinese Restaurant, the White Castle on West Main, where he stopped for hamburgers when on his paper route (five cents each or six for a quarter), and the Coney Island, run by the Levas brothers, friends from school days.

On one visit we were invited to have Sunday dinner with the Kavanaugh family on Ashland Avenue, and I met his longtime friends, Toby and his younger brother, Michael. After dinner Toby showed me the pool table in the basement that his father had bought the boys to "keep them out of trouble." They filled me in on the history of their early pool playing days.

Both Toby and Walter began their pool careers at that table. Toby went on to make his life's work running a poolroom, and Walter wrote *The Hustler*, based on his experiences. As young boys they watched the pros play billiards for big money at the Phoenix Hotel. Toby and Walter practiced the shots they learned from the big time players on the pool table in the Kavanaughs' basement. Walter was a fair player, but not as good as Toby because of a hand-to-eye coordination problem. When they thought they were ready, they took their game to small towns around Lexington such as Georgetown, Richmond, Paris, and Winchester and hustled the locals. This was in the days before pool halls were respectable. Once at a lecture at Eastern Kentucky University, Walter said that the pool hall of that day was "a way for boys to break from their mothers."

While I walked around with Walter while he smoked, he told me about the writing course he had attended the summer before we met at the University of Kentucky. A. B. Guthrie, Jr., author of *The Big Sky* and the screenplay for the movie *Shane*, was the teacher. Walter told me that after the encouragement he received in the writing class, he sent three of his stories to *The Saturday Evening Post.* He had added a note that if they didn't want the stories it would be his last attempt at trying to sell to *The Post.* One of the submissions was a children's story, "Cobweb," a fantasy about a fairy that cursed.

Walter saved one of the rejection letters from that submission. Stuart Rose, the editor, responded that he liked "Cobweb," but that it was "a bit too soft." Mr. Rose warned Walter that he was being foolish to send out stories only once. "Some people send out stories forty or fifty times before they get published," he wrote. Then he encouraged Walter this way: "We recognize your talent, and if you keep on writing, it is only a matter of time until you commence selling stories to us."

When Walter told me he was going to be a writer, I didn't appreciate his contacts with big time magazines and New York publishers. To me these were just the dreams of a young man; he was a high school English teacher. I had never known anyone who wrote anything more significant than an article for the local newspaper. I also had a dream then—I was going to become a foreign missionary. In reality we were in Carlisle, Kentucky, teaching in a small high school, selling popcorn and coffee at football games. The team was so small that if a player got hurt, there was no one to replace him.

"Cobweb" got lost somewhere along the way and was one of the few stories Walter wrote that was never published.

Another story from that writing class had more luck than "Cobweb" did. Helen Everitt, a New York agent, had been a guest in Mr. Guthrie's class and liked Walter's story "The Best in the Country." Later, Mr. Guthrie suggested that Walter send the story to her. She, in turn, forwarded the story to Kenneth Littauer, another New York agent, and he agreed to try to sell it.

Mid-October, school was closed for a teachers' meeting in Lexington, and with our second paycheck we went shopping. I went to a nice dress shop and I got a new brown tweed coat, a royal blue two-piece knit dress that was fashionable at the time, and brown pumps. Most everything in my wardrobe I had made myself. I got Mother a blouse and Daddy a pair of shoes. Since I brought my food from the farm and rent was very little, I felt very rich and money went a long way in 1952. Walter bought two jackets–a brown one and a blue plaid that he modeled in Walgreen's Drug Store. We went our separate ways–me to the farm to visit my parents and he to visit Toby's poolroom and spend the weekend in his Aunt Sallie's basement.

On Monday, Walter didn't return to school and his aunt called the principal to say he had pneumonia and would not be back for a week. I wrote him a letter telling of the amusing happenings of our mutual freshman girl students. The class and I had made candy using some Karo Syrup in the cabinet that proved to be spoiled. It gave all of us diarrhea. Claudia, who had a real taste for sweets, had pigged out on it and spent most of the next class period in the bathroom.

On Saturday afternoon, Walter returned on the bus and came directly to Mrs. Cash's house where I was living. He had my letter with him, corrected with his red marking pencil. "I had nothing else to read," he said.

It was a warm fall day, and we took a walk down a country road. He asked me to marry him. It seemed the natural thing to do. I said, "Yes."

Thanksgiving, we went to visit our parents who all happened to live in Madison County. His parents lived in Richmond and my parents lived seven miles away on a farm near Union City. There were some signals on that first visit to our parents that our relationship would have some rough spots. We were stepping into Main Street in Lexington and Walter said, "You know I am not going to stop drinking."

He made some remarks under his breath about the worth of old people after we visited my aging grandparents whom I dearly loved. I think his parents thought their son's resources were too few to think about marriage and would rather he had chosen a more glamorous girl from a more sophisticated background. As youth has a way of doing, we ignored the warning signs and continued with our lives as two lonely people in a small town.

On that visit I heard the Tevis family history, a story I would hear many times. They had had hard times but were proud of their origins. Walter's father was a self-educated man, descended from the first families of Madison County, Kentucky. When he was on his own, he went to Oakland, California, to be an appraiser of large companies. Walter's mother, Betty, the daughter of an upstate New York Presbyterian minister, was an elementary school teacher. They met on a train, married, went to live in sunny California, and soon afterwards had two children–Betty Jean and Walter.

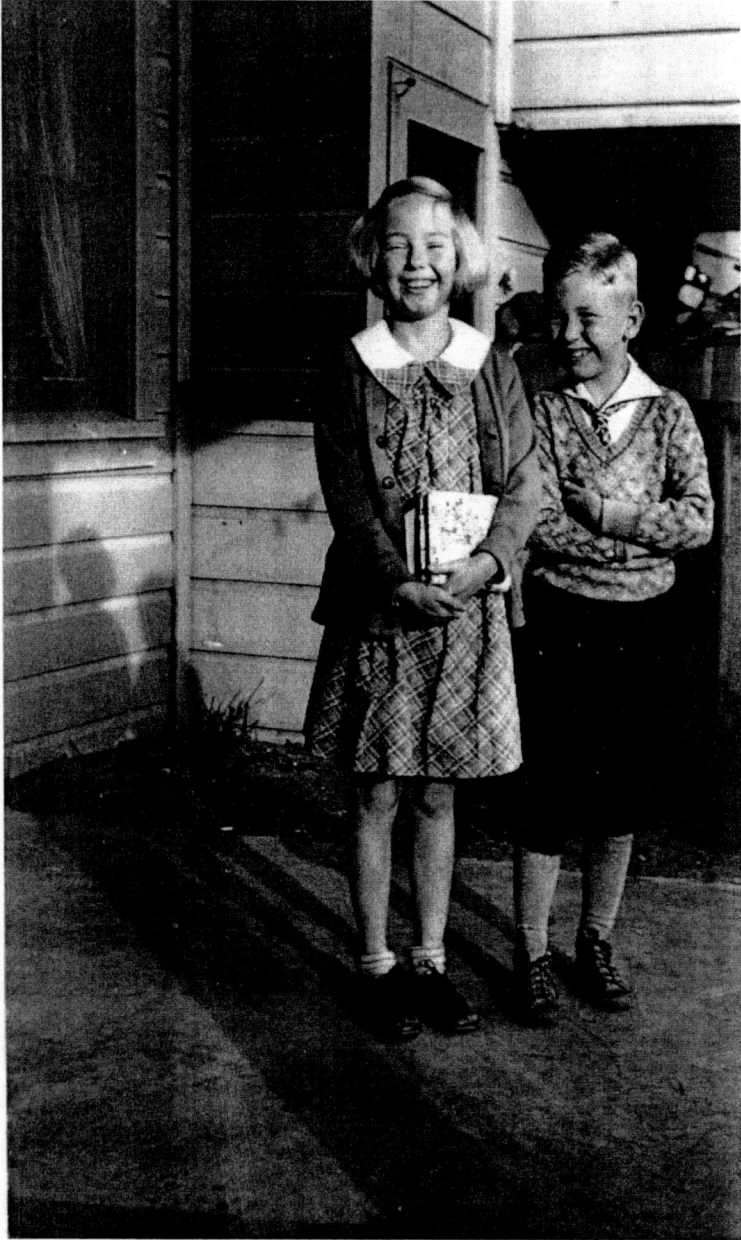

Life in California is good.
Sister Betty and Walter

Life was good for the Tevis family in Oakland until the Depression came; money ran out so they decided to return to Kentucky to live with Mr. Tevis' older sister, Sallie. The move was complicated because at the time, ten-year-old Walter was ill from a bad attack of measles that was followed by a strep throat that led to rheumatic fever. The lady doctor who was treating Walter told the family that if he was her child she would leave him in the Stanford University hospital where he would receive the best of free medical care. It was a difficult decision to make; but considering the long ride across country, the lack of money, the cost of treatment, and the uncertain living conditions when they arrived in Kentucky, they decided to leave Walter behind.

This is the way he always related the story to me. He was flat on a hospital bed, wrapped in a gray, scratchy wool blanket. Over him was put a kind of homemade machine of some sort of steel. It was a half-cylinder that covered his body from neck to ankles. They strapped his hands to his sides so he wouldn't break the light bulbs in the box that raised his internal temperature to 107 degrees and caused him to have convulsions.

Every two weeks they applied the treatment. There was no clock in the room, and when he would ask the time, the attendant would be cross with him. He tried to count off the time in his head, a second at a time. He had a picture in his mind of his Daddy bringing him a glass of water. He prayed to die.

The treatment was a project of the doctor who had advised the family to leave Walter in the hospital. She had Walter's parents sign to authorize the treatment. The treatment was later abandoned as too dangerous.

Walter was kept in bed for one year. The family wrote regularly, and he had regular visits from a family friend, Jenny. There were other children in the room, one being a bully. To keep the patients quiet, they were given phenobarbital, which

Walter loved. He believed that is where he got his liking for alcohol.

Walter always talked of the experience as if it had happened to someone else. In his head he was aware that it had a great effect on his life, and during the time I knew him he was never able to deal with the pain. After he went to New York, he used his memories as the basis of *Queen's Gambit*. This quote from that book shows how closely the fictional character's experience matched Walter's own. "Beth Harmon is sent to the Methuen Home. A plain, shy, frightened little girl, she survives on the tranquilizers the Home doles out to keep the children easier to handle."

The physical scars left from the illness were a weakened heart and some uncontrolled movements of his hands and body called St. Vitus' Dance. Other than not being active in sports, which he didn't care about anyway, his adult lifestyle was not affected. What the experience did to his mental life is another story.

The nurses in the hospital would talk to Walter about the wonderful blue grass he would soon be seeing. His dream of horse races and fancy living was soon shattered. Walter told me stories that showed the big changes that happened to his family while he was in the hospital.

When Walter was dismissed, his parents had no money for his train ticket. The family friend, Jenny, who had visited Walter regularly in the hospital, purchased the ticket, and Mrs. Tevis sent her diamond engagement ring for security. Eventually she was able to repay the debt and get the ring back. At her death, my mother-in-law left me that ring in her will.

When Walter told me stories from his childhood, he always used the family nicknames. Everyone in Walter's family had nicknames. Jas for Mr. Tevis, and Barney for Walter are names that stuck for a lifetime within the family. The man, Walter, remembered the boy, Barney, doing happy things with his father, Jas, when they lived in California. He recalled several highlights from that time–like the good time he and Jas had gathering potatoes that grew on the town dump. Another special memory was the time they went to a house to buy Barney shoes that were advertised in the newspaper.

When Walter got to Kentucky, things had changed. His mother had given up her bridge playing days to become a housekeeper in her sister-in-law's home. Mr. Tevis had a job as a truck driver for a mattress company. His father had become a silent, defeated man who left the rearing of his son to his mother. Writers of the day refer to such experiences as "the scars of the Depression."

Walter had changed too. After a year in the hospital, he was a tall, skinny eleven-year-old with low self-esteem. He felt like an alien. That boy later became Newton in *The Man Who Fell to Earth*. Walter's memories of California became the planet Anthea.

He attended the sixth grade in a tough neighborhood. His mother considered him to be a "very bright semi-invalid," and she kept him out of gym classes. Being smart and frail made Walter the target of bullies, and he was regularly beaten up by tough boys. Things improved when he became friends with Toby and Michael Kavanaugh. Being doctor's sons, their mother thought they should attend a private school, not the roughest school in town. Their father, however, insisted they go to the local school to toughen them up. Their mother compromised by sending them in a chauffeured car. After making friends with the Kavanaughs, Walter spent much of his time at their house–a house with a pool table.

A few years after Walter got to Kentucky, Mr. Tevis got a better job as a traffic manager at the Blue Grass Ordinance Depot in Madison County, and the family moved to Richmond. There, Walter enrolled as a junior at Madison Model High School.

Walter's health improved over the years in Kentucky, and he was fit enough to join the Navy at seventeen. When I met him, he appeared healthy except for a slight tremor in his hand when he lighted a cigarette.

When I met Walter's parents on that first visit after we got engaged, I could see that his mother was a talker and his dad was the silent type. He didn't approve of his son's being a teacher–considering it women's work. Walter's father often mentioned that he did admire the people he read about in *Time* magazine. Walter's enjoyment of his writing success was tainted by disappointment that his father died before *The Hustler* became a movie and was reviewed in *Time* magazine. He never stopped longing for his father's approval. The night after his father's funeral he put his head under the covers and sobbed.

I had been reared on a small farm in the community of Union City, where we were very active in my mother's Baptist church and my dad's Methodist church at Doylesville, seven miles on down the road. I had a sister, Lucy, eight years older. We helped with the farm chores, and for my first three years in school, before a bus came within a mile of our house, we rode on horseback to school. With a background of farming and church, the opportunities open to young girls were marriage, nursing, or teaching. My sister chose home economics and became a home demonstration agent. She married Johnny Pittman, a soldier she met at the U.S.O. during her first year of employment.

As the time for my graduation from high school came nearer, I was very concerned about what I was going to do with my life. Several of my friends were getting married, but this possibility had no interest for me at the time. Every year on Homecoming Day at my dad's church, guest singers came to sing. One homecoming, a male quartet came from nearby Asbury College. When they sang, "Oh, Happy Day. Oh Happy Day, when Jesus washed my sins away . . ." I decided that if people in college sang like that, I had to go, too. I convinced my parents to let me go to Georgetown Baptist College, a few miles past Lexington.

It was not easy for my parents to send me to college. They postponed things such as an indoor bathroom and a new car, continuing to drive their old farm truck to save enough to pay my fees. Mother was happy that I was going to college as she had never had the privilege. She helped me collect the things I would need — clothes, sheets, bedspread, and rugs for my dorm room.

At Georgetown Baptist College it wasn't long before I realized there were two choices for me there: become a minister or marry one. My sophomore year I returned to our hometown of Richmond and enrolled at Eastern State University in home economics.

I made friends at Eastern and ran with a group of students with backgrounds similar to mine. My junior year I was elected president of the Baptist Student Union on campus. Although there were boys in the group, we didn't often pair off in couples. We found the arrangement very comfortable. Near graduation some of the couples did marry, and I could have also, but I was enjoying my independence and was looking forward to my first teaching position. However, leaving the security of class friends and the protective college life was a bit frightening.

Bob Davis, superintendent of Carlisle High School, always came to Miss Burrier, head of the Home Economics Department, when he needed a new teacher. The girl he had hired before me had gotten pregnant out of wedlock before the school year was over. Miss Burrier recommended me as the first choice of her "girls," trusting that a good Baptist girl could get through the year safely.

Daddy drove me over to Carlisle, about thirty miles from Lexington, for the interview. It was a clean, little farming community, built around the courthouse square with the usual stores common to such Kentucky towns. Mr. Davis showed us around the school — an old, well-kept building containing all twelve grades. The Home Economics room was in the basement. He said I would have about thirty-five girls in my classes, and I felt this was a manageable size for a first-year teacher. He sent me downtown to a jewelry store to meet the owner Mr. Facemeyer, president of the school board.

He was an affable gentleman and pointed out some of the advantages of living in his town, such as being close to Lexington being on a bus line, and having a number of churches. He explained that Mr. Davis, though a very decent man, did have a temper and some teachers did not like to work for him. I was not to be quickly offended. He told this story to illustrate his point:

Mr. Davis took pride in his school, and each year he had the janitor give the wooden floors another coat of varnish until they shone like glass. One year a fourth grade student walked through the hall leaving muddy tracks from the front door right up to his desk. Mr. Davis took a bucket of water and a rag, tracked the culprit to his seat, and gave loud instructions to clean up the footprints. The new teacher took offense that Mr. Davis had interrupted her class in this manner.

Mr. Facemyer said I could have the position as Home Economics teacher if I wanted it for $195 per month.

I got a room with a widow lady, Mrs. Cash, who rented to single girls. It wasn't long before the newness of the place wore off, and life in Carlisle was not much different from my home community, Union City. I soon discovered that I was single in a married society. I went to church where I was treated very kindly, and a couple of the younger married ladies were especially friendly. The other place in town where I could visit was the drug store where the students hung out. Besides me, there were only two other single people on the faculty: Carroll Hall and Walter Tevis. Carroll was the band leader in his second year and dating a local girl, Kay Hall. Walter was the English teacher and lived in a small trailer with another fellow. They got their water from the church next door.

Jamie Tevis

Starting a life together in Carlisle, Kentucky.
Jamie and Walter, two young teachers.

I got along fine with Mr. Davis and with the older women that made up most of the small faculty. Saturday afternoons were deadly quiet and lonely for a single person, so Mr. Davis and his wife often asked me to accompany them for drives to Lexington, through the peaceful, rolling fields of bluegrass, with grazing race horses, black barns, and rock fences. Then they treated me to dinner in a restaurant. It wasn't until later that Mr. Davis' temper changed my life.

When I told my parents I was getting married to a fellow teacher, Walter Tevis, the only question they asked was, "Does he drink?" I had lived such a sheltered life that I didn't know the consequences of alcoholism—never having known an alcoholic personally. When my parents asked me about drinking, I reasoned that almost everyone in the larger world drank socially. I would never get married if I went by my parents' conservative beliefs. I told them the biggest lie of my life and answered, "No."

Carlisle, Kentucky (December 1952- June 1953)

We married in Carlisle before Christmas vacation, less than four months after we met. Our wedding ceremony was a small affair performed in a Baptist church by the local minister. Toby Kavanaugh was Walter's best man. Toby's brother, Michael, and Evan Bullock were ushers, and two of my girlfriends, Audrey Covington and Patsy Sizemore, were my attendants. Walter's Aunt Sallie and both sets of parents were there, along with a handful of students and friends. Toby drove us to Lexington where we had drinks at the Chevy Chase restaurant before we caught the train for Louisville.

At the end of our short honeymoon, we returned to Carlisle and set up housekeeping in a two-room apartment upstairs in the house of a pleasant local lady. We cooked on a hot plate, got water from the bathroom for dishes, and took showers by going through the lady's bedroom. We painted the kitchen wall flame red, and Walter decorated it with fairies peeping around the door facing. We thought it a wonderful, cozy place. Two weeks after we were married we were back in a classroom.

In the spring of 1953, a letter from Kenneth Littauer came that marked the beginning of Walter's professional writing career. The letter said that *Esquire* magazine had accepted "The Best in the Country" for $350 and that the check would be coming soon. I remember that Mr. Littauer wrote that he wished it could have been more and that it was a "miserable sum." For teachers with a salary of $200 a month, $350 was not a miserable sum.

The sale of "The Best in the Country" established Kenneth as Walter's New York agent.

This sale did not make us rich, but it meant that Walter had broken into the magazine market and that he now had an agent. I framed the letter and hung it where all could see, especially my parents. To celebrate, Walter invited his classes and our single faculty friends for a picnic. It rained, so we had potato chips and hot dogs in our living room. The sophomores, who called Walter "Ichabod Crane" behind his back, began to take their teacher more seriously and worked a little harder on their essays. My parents also began to take a different view of their son-in-law.

Walter had no teaching certificates, so his contract could not be renewed until the first day of school, in case someone with a degree showed up and applied for the job. Then in May 1953, just before school was out, we found out that Walter would not be hired for the next year at Carlisle because of a run-in with the principal.

Walter was director of the junior-senior play, and one of the props was a couch from the basement teachers' lounge. After the play he had a couple of strong boys carry it back to the basement, lifting it over the seats in the auditorium. Principal Davis saw that a leg was missing and shouted at Walter, "You . . .You broke the leg off my couch!"

"Sir, I did not. It was off when we borrowed it. We put a book under it for support," Walter calmly answered.

Mr. Davis gave a few more oaths and shouted, "You are fired!"

It never occurred to me to stay in Carlisle and keep my home economics position while Walter went to find work. "Whither thou goest, I go" was what a wife did in those days. To improve our employment prospects, we decided to use our last meager paychecks and the money from wedding gifts to enroll in graduate school at the University of Kentucky in Lexington for the summer term.

The last week of the summer session, I was finishing a project with another woman in our class. "I have been having a stomach ache and not feeling well," I told her.

"Maybe you are pregnant," she casually answered. I went to the school doctor and it was true. I came home and told Walter. His response was, "Maybe it will go away." It didn't go away and has proven over the years that sometimes unplanned events are the biggest blessings in life.

At the end of summer school I was three months pregnant, money was running out, and we had no choice but to go to my parents on the farm. Before we left Lexington, I walked to the neighborhood grocery and paid our bill with the little that was left in our checking account. Walter and I were discussing our lack of funds when my dad's footsteps were heard on the stairs. We loaded our few possessions in his car and drove to the farm in Union City. We planned to spend only a month until Walter could be hired. Somewhere there had to be a school that needed an English teacher–even one without a teaching certificate.

My parents were not very pleased that they had sent a daughter out into the world to support herself, only to have her come home broke and pregnant at the end of summer with no job and an unemployed husband who had to wait until opening day of school to be considered for a teaching position.

"Don't worry, I'm going to be a writer and sell short stories that bring thousands of dollars," Walter told my mother.

Both of my parents always treated Walter very well. They only showed me their anger and frustration about our situation. They thought of him as a teacher, not a writer.

Irvine, Kentucky (Fall 1953-Summer 1955)

Walter did get another teaching job, his fourth, in a little Kentucky town, Irvine. My mother found it for him. She was going to a church conference and Walter told her, "Ask around and see if they need an English teacher."

She came back with the happy news that indeed there was a job opening in Irvine City High School. The arrangements were made by phone. The salary was $185 a month with a small four-room house at the end of the football field that could be rented for $30 a month. My dad drove us in his truck, and we gathered furnishings on the way: a bed and breakfast set from Walter's mother's basement, bedding and kitchen things from my mother, and–on credit from a second-hand store–a refrigerator and a stove with a door that had to be propped with a chair. As the furnishings were being unloaded, the principal drove up in the yard and said we might not want to stay as the students were on strike over losing their football coach, and he didn't know how long before it would be settled. In spite of the strike, the situation looked more hopeful than returning to my parents, so we chose to stay.

The bed was set up with its thin cotton mattress. Nauseated from my four months of pregnancy, I fell on the bed, and my dad drove away. I didn't even have a broom to sweep the cracked linoleum.

After a while, Walter, always cheerful, suggested we walk the three blocks to town and borrow $25 from the credit union for groceries. At the drugstore while we were drinking five-cent Cokes, he said, "This is the largest town I have taught in. It has two movie theaters." That did not impress me. My idea of success was to go toward Richmond and the Bluegrass, not moving from school to school in small mountain towns. An ambulance came through with its siren blasting, bringing someone from Beattyville on the way to Lexington–to the nearest hospital, twenty miles farther. It reminded me how far we were from the life I had hoped for. Later Walter would speak of the fact that the dry towns he taught in helped keep his drinking under control.

School opened soon, and we made friends with an older neighbor couple, Beulah and T.G Richmond. Beulah let me use her sewing machine, and T.J. made Walter feel free to work in his well-stocked woodworking shop. He was delighted to be able to use skills he had learned in the Navy as carpenter's mate, and he made a cradle for the coming baby and a cobbler's bench coffee table for my mother.

Irvine was a lovely little mountain town, and in the fall the hills around us were beautiful. For a special treat we took the cab for the two-mile ride to Ravina, a little railroad town with a super drugstore. Since there was no restaurant in Irvine and our funds were low, another treat for us was to have a roast beef and gravy sandwich at the Greyhound bus station.

Life was pleasant but a little lonely, and we had no car to get away on weekends. We did have some friends, but one has to be born into a small town such as Irvine to be really one of them. We were considered a little weird, but one time they came to Walter for aid because we were different. The police had picked up a man for loitering. They couldn't get the man to talk and brought him to the high school to see "that strange young fellow who knows a lot." "Let's see if he can get him to talk," they reasoned. Walter spoke no language other than English, and he was unsuccessful in his attempts to get the man to speak. Walter suspected the man was a Mexican farm worker. The next day the local paper carried a small article. "Man Found Dead in Madison County." The man had been found hanging from a tree with a wire around his neck. He was identified by a military service record in his pocket, and had $81.62 in money, a bus ticket to the next town, and a Kentucky fishing license. We knew he was the depressed and lonely man brought to Walter the day before. We were sad that no one could help him.

On a number of occasions in Irvine we had happy visits from Frank Mathias, an old college friend of Walter's. Frank had the job of driving through mountain counties, stocking the small grocery stores with Kent cigarettes after they first came on the market. About once a month his route brought him through Irvine, and he stopped by our house bringing beer and supplying Walter with cigarette samples. At Frank's suggestion I prepared the same simple but delicious dinner each time he came. I put a can of sauerkraut in a casserole, covered it with spare ribs, and baked it in the oven for one hour with greased baking potatoes. It was the perfect fall meal when the hills were turning yellow and bronze and frost was in the air. Walter and Frank always talked into the night.

Several years later we returned to Irvine and drove by to see the little house we had lived in. When we stopped to speak to the neighbors next door, we were reminded that we had been outsiders there.

"Will, see the birds. See the cars."
Baby Will and Jamie.

"Oh, yes. I remember you all. You were them people who ate the weeds that grew by the fence posts on the road," was our greeting. Our former neighbor was remembering that in the spring we had enjoyed gathering the tender young asparagus plants that grew wild where the birds had scattered the seed. The neighbors had a huge asparagus bed that they treated as a shrub. We always looked on it with envy as we gathered our few stalks.

The Birth of Will (March 8, 1954)

Our son was born in Richmond, Kentucky, in Pattie A. Clay Hospital on March 8, 1954. Walter was teaching at Irvine High School, and we still lived in the four-room house at the end of the football field.

I went to bed about 10 o'clock on Sunday night, and Walter was reading in the next room. After a while I said, "The time has come. Go get Dr. Markham." It was agreed that the doctor would examine me to determine if it was time to go over to Richmond to the hospital, about twenty miles away. Dr. Markham said I was ready and went for his car. I sat in the living room on my suitcase waiting for his return, panic-struck. As the contractions got closer together I said, "I can't go through with this." The soon-to-be father said, "It's too late to think about that now."

Dr. Markham drove us to Richmond; I sat between the two men. At the hospital the nurse gave me an enema. I sat on a pot, gripping the iron bed rail, in such pain until I believed I was bending the rail. When I got back in bed, the nurse put a gas mask over my face to relieve the pains. She told Walter to hold the mask over my face whenever I asked for it. He almost passed out and had to go out for a smoke and a walk down the hall.

About 6 o'clock on Monday morning, a nine-pound boy came into the world. He had a head of fine, black hair about two inches long, and the fat on his face had been compressed into jowls. Back in the room, the young father, who had never seen a newborn, said, "It is the ugliest baby I have ever seen."

I had seen lots of newborns and said, "He is a beautiful baby." I was so proud to have a boy. In the delivery room, I had said, "He is the first boy to be born into the family in fifty-four years." I knew my dad would be pleased. We decided to name him William Thomas, after his great-grandfather who had been one of Morgan's Raiders during the Civil War. "We will call him Will," we agreed.

His grandparents, Betty and Walter Stone Tevis, Lloyd and Fannie Griggs, and his great-grandmother Cora all came to see the new baby. Betty brought a little pink cap and an embroidered coat that had been fashionable in her time. Her son Walter had worn such an outfit when he went home from the California hospital in 1928. Someone brought a jar of custard and grapes for me.

I stayed in the hospital a week, and Walter returned to Irvine to teach his English classes. Someone sold him a life insurance policy for the baby for $36 per year that could be cashed when he was eighteen and would be worth $1000.

On Friday, Walter returned to collect his family. The nurse brought the baby from the nursery and put him on the bed for the new father to dress. He handled Will as though the child would break as he dressed him in the silly pink outfit.

Grandmother Betty came to the hospital to see the baby in the outfit she had made him. My father, Lloyd, came to pick up the new family and took us to the farm where we would spend the weekend together before Walter went back to Irvine. I put the baby to sleep for the night in a bassinet by my side of the bed. In the night I checked on him and found that he had kicked off the covers and his fat little legs were as cold as a toad. Believing I had given him a chill, I took him into the bed between Walter and me. We were afraid to move for fear of smothering him.

So, after fourteen months, the couple who had met in Carlisle was now a family of three. Walter signed a contract to teach a second year in Irvine.

At home, Walter set up an office in one of the rooms and kept Will out by barring the door with a chair. We replaced the space heater that had to be turned off at night with a larger gas stove that heated all the house. Walter wrote short stories and came home from school mid-morning for a cup of coffee and to see if there was a letter from his agent. My dad came by one day and saw me washing diapers in the sink. He got me a wringer washing machine from the secondhand store. While doing the washing and housework, I listened to Arthur Godfrey and to the McCarthy hearings on our little green radio. A close neighbor, Jane Scott, had a baby Will's age, and we enjoyed pushing their strollers the few blocks to town, where Jane and I drank Cokes at the drugstore.

When Will was old enough to sit up, Walter dressed him in red pants and sweater and carried him on his shoulders around the football field. I got an afternoon job teaching English in the middle school, and the lady across the road kept Will. As I carried him across the yard to her house, I said, "See the birds. See the cars." One day, he said his first sentence "See car." I'm sure it meant to him the whole lovely outdoor world. When he could sit alone, we played his favorite game—I would sneeze, and he would laugh until he fell over onto the floor.

As a toddler, he learned he could open the refrigerator door. He would take out an egg in each hand and run through the house, pressing them against his chest. I replaced the eggs with lemons. While we ate dinner, Will sat on the floor and stacked the cans from a low cupboard.

When Will was a toddler, Mr. Tevis had lung cancer, so he and Mrs. Tevis drove over to Lexington every Saturday for his treatments, and Mrs. Tevis would dash into our house for a few minutes to see Will. She always brought a little gift in her hand and would say, "Isn't this nice?" One time after she made her whirlwind visit, Will looked around for her and said, "Where 'Nice' go?" The name stuck, and even though she has been gone for many years, we still refer to her as "Nice."

Later we often recalled those good days when we were independent and starting our family. I realize now that the two years we had in Irvine were the happiest of our marriage because Walter's drinking was under control in that dry town.

Walter and Money

Walter sometimes got letters of encouragement, and in 1955 he sold a story to *Collier's* magazine. We left the baby with my mother as soon as school was out in the spring, and Toby took us to the airport for a trip to New York. It was our first plane ride and my first trip to a big city. Many years later we would return for the movie openings of *The Hustler* and *The Man Who Fell to Earth*.

In the plane on the way to New York, Walter told me about his other trips to the Big Apple. In the summers when Walter and Toby were schoolboys, they had worked at the stockyards, driving sheep. They recalled using a goat to lead the sheep, paying the goat for her help with cigarettes. With the money he earned, he rode the bus to New York to spend a few weeks visiting his Aunt Myra on Park Avenue before school began.

At one time she had been married to a millionaire and had played bridge with such folk as Ernest Hemingway and Ezra Pound. During the Depression she lost her money and the apartment building she had owned. At the time Walter visited her, she was permitted to live in the maid's apartment on the whole top floor of the Park Avenue building overlooking Central Park. Aunt Myra was quite happy wearing overalls and working as a riveter in a defense plant during World War II. In spite of her reduced standard of living, she introduced Walter to the pleasure of eating in good restaurants and gave him a taste of New York life. Myra had died the year before I came into the family. Walter was the first relative to realize that Myra was paranoid. When she heard someone whistle she had thought it was the FBI after her. She heard someone whistle in the bank lobby, had a stroke, and died.

On our visit we didn't have the money to live in high style. We ate our meals at dreary Child's restaurants and the Automat and stayed in the relatively inexpensive Plymouth Hotel. On arrival Walter could not wait a minute to show me New York; we immediately left our bags at the hotel and set out on foot to see the sights walking against the shoulder-to-shoulder rush-hour traffic. No one had prepared me for having to step over the homeless people lying on the street. To get out of the traffic we went into Hector's Cafeteria. The line was moving a mile a minute and the people behind the counter couldn't understand my Kentucky accent. Walter would try to tell the waiters what I wanted and they barked back, "The lady will have to speak for herself." My first meal in New York was a glass of iced tea and bread without butter.

Walter took me to the regular attractions–The Rockettes, the Statue of Liberty–but what I enjoyed most were the Broadway shows. The ones I remember best were *Solid Gold Cadillac*, *Tea House of the August Moon*, and *Tea and Sympathy*. However, the most exciting part of the trip for Walter was when we were having lunch with his agent Kenneth, and he encouraged Walter to enlarge "The Best in the Country" into a novel.

When my parents picked us up at the airport with the baby, we had one nickel between us. Life with Walter was full of adventure but a little too risky for my taste, and I had felt very guilty about having left a new baby. I decided that my role in the marriage would have to be that of the heavy, the responsible one. When we went to see *The Hustler* years later, there I was on the screen in the character of Charlie. I felt so exposed I wanted to crawl under the seat.

One might think that Walter's writing made him wealthy. It didn't. We bought older houses that needed lots of work and bought only one new car. Mostly we lived on Walter's teaching salary.

Walter seemed to have a deep aversion to saving. His mother told him that if he would invest fifteen percent of each magazine and book sale, he would build up a sizable savings account. I attribute Walter's attitude towards money as a reaction to being a child of the Depression and as a rebellion against living with his frugal Aunt Sallie, his father's sister. She was always saving, putting newspapers on the kitchen floor after mopping, putting covers on the furniture, etc. (In her defense, she shared her home with her sister Myra and with her brother's family when they came to her in need.) Walter admired the way his Aunt Myra had handled money. Aunt Myra had lost her apartment house overlooking Central Park, but she had lived her life in style–enjoying money while she had it.

Twenty years later, Walter showed he still was willing to spend it all. When Walter left for New York, all he had to take with him were two twenty-year-old book rights and one book in the making. He took a gamble that he could write again. By cutting off his relationship with Ohio University, his retirement plan and health insurance were terminated. All or nothing was his game. (Walter also showed his tendency to take excessive risks when he played cards. Donald Justice, a faculty friend who played poker with Walter while in graduate school in Iowa said, "Here was this man who wrote this book about gambling who was the worst poker player I ever saw.")

Walter seemed unable to keep to a budget. Even if we made a budget, he didn't follow it. Easy come–easy go was his attitude. When we had to work at making ends meet, I kept the household accounts. When times were easier, he paid the bills. When we were settled in Athens, Ohio, years after the time we returned to Kentucky from New York with only a nickel, I brought home my first paycheck from a new job after many years as a housewife. Walter casually said, "Deposit it in the checking account." He had always been generous with the money he earned, but I could not see $800 added to the checking account with no plans for how it would be spent. I knew it would just disappear. I wanted to see what my money bought, so we decided I would deposit the money in a bank account in my name. Our daughter Julie was taking music lessons, so I purchased a Yamaha piano and paid for our plane tickets to London with my first paychecks from that job. Walter didn't like it. Men seem to relate money to manhood, and Walter was no different, but I held my ground, and he didn't make too big a fuss.

We never depended on the writing income for living expenses; instead, we bought special things with it or traveled. I remember that I wrote a list of things to buy on the back of the letter of acceptance from *The Saturday Evening Post* for a short story called "William." I planned to buy curtain rods, curtains, pans, a clothes hamper, sheets, and towels. The letter offered $1,250, which was about equal to six months of a teacher's salary. The things listed on the back of the letter would make our house a little more cheerful. Groceries cost about $8 a bag, and 50 cents paid the ride home in a cab. When the check came we purchased the items on the list. There was even enough money for two airline tickets to New York and for a maple bed with a matching chest of drawers ($300). I sleep in that bed every night.

We were very frugal and didn't own a car. By the first year of our marriage, I was shopping and preparing the meals with skills learned in home economics classes. I never cared for oatmeal, though Walter could survive on it. Two other foods he had learned to prepare were canned Dinty Moore Beef Stew

*Walter in his office at the Kentucky Highway
Department where he wrote the Hustler.*

and macaroni and cheese.

Walter was teaching in northern Kentucky at a branch of the University of Kentucky when *The Hustler* was sold to the movies. With the money from the sale, Walter earned a Master of Fine Arts degree from Iowa and financed nine months in Mexico. A friend once gave me a tube of lipstick for my birthday, saying she never knew anybody who had only one. I was a frugal shopper. Walter took it for granted that he would buy two bottles of wine a day and cigarettes. He had two other extravagant habits.

Walter's second extravagant habit was eating in fancy restaurants. When he ate out with others, he was always generous about picking up the checks. At home I prepared Walter plain, good home cooking which he appreciated when he was sober. I recall that late in his life, after we had separated, he asked me for my meatloaf recipe. I wrote it on a table napkin for him.

Walter's free-spending ways went against my strong conservative tendencies. I had to fight against his foolish financial habits to keep the family afloat. I learned to put a little money aside (like Charlie in *The Hustler*), so I always had something for an emergency. I also recognize, however, that Walter's daring ways enhanced my life greatly. The conservative me would never have seen the sights of Broadway. Nor would I have flown to London and seen the Changing of the Guard, the Tower of London, and the Queen of England. It was Walter's daring that let me live in Mexico for nine months. Without Walter, I might never have lived outside of Kentucky. Because of Walter, I learned that there are good and wonderful people wherever we call home. I might have married a dull man.

We Move from Irvine to Lexington–With Some Detours

We had two good years in Irvine, but at the end of the second we decided to return to Lexington where Walter could work toward a master's degree in English to be qualified for a more permanent job. Before we got moved, a special opportunity came up for Walter. Toby's mother went to Europe every summer, but could never get her sons to go with her, and she told Walter, "If you can convince Toby and Michael to go, I'll pay your way." I wished the offer had come before we were married, but it was an opportunity too good to let pass. Walter convinced the brothers to go, borrowed money from the credit union, and went to Europe for the summer of 1955. Will and I went to stay with my parents on the farm.

Lexington, Kentucky (Fall 1955-Fall 1958)

After Walter got back from six weeks in Europe, he found an apartment in a comfortable, older house on Kentucky Avenue in Lexington. It was near my cousin Mary Boyd and her husband, Turley, around the corner from Chevy Chase where we could walk to a movie theater. After being so isolated in Irvine, we really enjoyed city life.

For several weeks at the end of the summer, Walter worked for Toby in his pool hall. Unfortunately, rather than bringing home money from his hours at Toby's poolroom, Walter ran up debt playing quarter games with the customers. He kept an account of what he owed in the cash register and promised to pay Toby when he sold stories to magazines. True to his word, he paid some from each story sale until the debt was paid.

Walter's natural inclination was to be careless with money, but his father had set him a good example. He believed it was a man's job to support his family and pay his debts.

With a small child and jobs to get to, the time had come to get a car. We went to the used car lot and picked out a dull green Studebaker with a pointed nose for $250. It was a great little car owned by a little old lady who had taken good care of it. Neither of us had a driver's license. Although I had driven machinery on the farm, Walter had never driven. The salesman parked the car in front of our house on Kentucky Avenue, and after Will was asleep we took practice trips around the block. One night Walter got too close to a fire hydrant and scraped the paint off the door. With his driving permit and his new delight in his driving skills, he invited another family to go with us to the lake. He managed to get the front tires in the lake and couldn't find reverse. Each time he would accelerate we would go a little farther into the water. Both of us did, eventually, become competent drivers.

Like his father, Walter liked to travel. On trips he was in charge, doing all the driving and playing games with the children. He was patient if we had to drive longer than planned to find lodging and never minded making stops. He had an innocence about him. Even on frequently traveled roads such as to Kentucky to see our parents, he anticipated running upon a new restaurant or shopping mall. On a long drive to Iowa, he was suffering from an acute ulcer, sipping milk and Maalox all the way, and yet he remained cheerful. When we got home he would say, "Everyone take in your suitcase." Inside the house he relaxed with a drink and turned responsibilities over to me.

In the fall of 1955, Walter quit working at Toby's and enrolled in classes at the University of Kentucky with a teaching fellowship. He was preparing himself to be a good provider for his family.

I got a job as a dietitian at Eastern State Mental Hospital. After Will had his fourth baby sitter in a single month, I decided to quit my job and to stay home with him. Walter could work a little harder to support us.

Walter Writes *The Hustler*

Walter finished his first master's degree in 1956 and got a job as an editor at the Kentucky Highway Department. With a steady income, we decided to look for a larger apartment and found a duplex on Delmont Drive on the edge of Lexington. It was fairly new with a warm basement where Walter set up his office. The best part for me was the garden. The house was built on land that had once been a tobacco patch, so it was very fertile and large enough for corn and pumpkins. Will loved to dig with me in the garden and find worms. We had a Little Golden Book that showed what went on under the soil that I read to him before nap time.

Walter was not a disciplined person, so the routine at the highway department was a great help in his writing. While sitting at a desk waiting for the engineers to turn in their reports, Walter found the discipline to write. Between editing assignments he produced several short stories for magazines: *Saturday Evening Post, Collier's,* etc. As his agent Kenneth had suggested, Walter enlarged "The Best in the Country," a story published in *Esquire,* and turned it into a novel, *The Hustler,* which eventually sold to the movies for $25,000.

Julia Anne Tevis Born (October 16, 1957)

Three and a half years after Will was born, while we lived in Lexington, I woke up around 5 A.M. with pains in my back and told Walter the time had come. We waited awhile and then called Dr. Welch. He told us to wait until the pains were closer together and regular before coming to his office.

We waited until about seven and then took Will over to Clay Avenue to my cousin Mary Boyd's house. I waved goodbye to him with tears in my eyes as he stood in the driveway wearing a little blue baseball cap. The fall had been mild and pleasant, and Will and I did something special every day while I waited for the new baby: gathering and hulling walnuts, riding the city bus to the end of the line and home again, going to downtown Lexington to get ice cream at Walgreen's drug store on Main Street. We had enjoyed these together and knew our lives would now be different.

Dr. Welch did deliveries at Good Samaritan Hospital (Baptist), across from his office, unless he had a delivery at Saint Joseph (Catholic) across town. Being a Baptist I preferred the Baptist hospital, but I agreed that if the doctor had another delivery at Saint Joseph's, I would go there. Dr. Welch examined me and said, "It is time. Go over to Saint Joseph Hospital." All I heard was the word "over," so we walked across the street to the Baptist hospital and signed in with my Blue Cross insurance card. The nurse took over and prepped me for delivery. After a time, Walter got restless with nothing to do but smoke, so he left. At that time men were not allowed past the waiting room. It was very quiet in the hospital and I was the only one in the room. The labor pains were coming regularly. The nurse said, "I wonder why Dr. Welch has not come or called?" She called him and he said, "What is she doing there? I want her over at Saint Joseph's. Is she able to go over there?"

I thought I could make it, so I got up and put on my brown maternity dress with white collar and cuffs, stopped at the desk for my Blue Cross card, and went through the big double doors to the exit. I was looking down twenty or more steps with only my Blue Cross card in hand, no coat to cover me if my water broke, no Walter in sight, and not a cent to get a taxi to Saint Joseph. Just as despair took over and a labor pain hit, I saw Walter crossing the street to come and check on my progress. He had gone to Toby's Pool Room to tell Toby the news.

How do you like my hair cut?
Young Julie.

Once at Saint Joseph events moved along and the pains got more regular. Dr. Welch lay on one bed and I lay on another, and we both napped, me between pains. When it was time, I was rolled into the delivery room. I assumed I would be given the same gas I had been given at Will's birth and come through feeling high and wonderful. But Dr. Welch used ether. I remember sinking down, down, and feeling I was dying. The nurse kept saying, "Push. Push one more time." I couldn't do anything more. I felt sad that this baby would never be born. I slipped away. I have never dreaded death after this experience. I believe that is what death will be like–a slipping away.

The next I knew, I was back in my room on my stomach with a crucifix on the wall above me, vomiting my insides out. At that unpleasant moment I had a visitor. My mother-in-law, Nice, came rushing through the door saying, "I have had the most awful time. I went to two hospitals trying to find you."

When I felt better, the nurse brought me a beautiful nine-pound girl and put her in my arms. "She will be Julia Anne, and we will call her Julie," Walter said. We had already chosen the name after some relative far back in the family who started the Science Hill School for girls near Louisville.

We took Julie home to Delmont Drive and then we were a family of four.

Julie was a pleasant baby with blond hair and brown eyes. I tried to keep her up for a late night feeding, but she gave it up and slept through the night anyway. In the morning she would wake us with her cooing.

We made good friends with our neighbors, the Thurmans. They had three children born in the same year–the twins, David and Johnny, and Sissy, who were playmates for Will. They often played Hide and Seek in the house. Will always hid in the toy box but couldn't wait to be found. He would jump out and say, "Here I is!" Walter came home for lunch from the highway department, and I often drove him back so I could have the car for errands.

Adlai Stevenson ran against Dwight Eisenhower, and it was the first time I voted. We got our first cat, and she had kittens in the back of the closet in my hatbox. They were Will's playmates while I shared my attention with Julie. A favorite toy was a large satin stuffed animal Nice had given him. He would try to lasso it with a rope and drag it down the stairs. One day he tried to do the same thing with a kitten. A salesman came by when I was feeding Julie and I asked him to rescue the kitten from the lasso. I remember him commenting, "Ma'am, children don't always do what we want them to do." Will had a fourth birthday in the Delmont house. Guests were David, Johnny, and Sissy from next door, Marsha and Mike Long, and Tony and Maria Canzonarie. I made them paper hats and cupcakes with green icing because it was near St. Patrick's Day.

The Hustler Lost!?

In 1957 Walter had been given an advance on *The Hustler* and felt he could afford to have the manuscript typed. One day we loaded Will into the Studebaker and went for a long ride in the country to see a recommended typist. We went back to pick up the manuscript on an agreed date and the house was empty, with no note telling of a forwarding address. A couple of months later, just after Julie was born, the typist (with no advance notice) brought the completed manuscript to our house. I had been quite worried, but Walter didn't seem to let it bother him. I don't think he had enough faith in what he had created to cause him to be overly concerned.

Walter immediately sent the manuscript to his agent, Kenneth, in New York. A couple of days later, he phoned mid-morning to say he would like Walter to come to New York to discuss the book. I phoned the good news to Walter at the Highway Department. He came home immediately, got on a plane, and was in New York before the day was over.

He returned with a stuffed kitten for Julie, a huge Lincoln Log set for Will, and an outfit for me. Best of all, he had the contract for *The Hustler* (called "In a Green Shade" at that point) and a $1000 advance.

We bought a twenty-one inch blond television set to celebrate *The Hustler*'s publication. Every night there were live dramas. Two years later, on December 13, 1959, we were thrilled to watch one of Walter's stories on "The Loretta Young Show."

The job at the Highway Department was perfect for Walter's writing career. However, he didn't like sitting at a desk all day, so when he heard of a teaching position he jumped at it.

Erlanger, Kentucky (Fall 1958-Summer 1959)

Walter got a job offer to teach English at the University of Kentucky branch in Covington across the river from Cincinnati. In the fall of 1958 we moved to the nearby town of Erlanger.

After Julie was born, I had postpartum depression that lasted for two years. The Russians had put Sputnik into space, and I thought, "Why have I brought this child into the world who will never have a chance to grow up and could have a bomb dropped on her head at any time?" It was a dark fear that invaded my life.

Walter went to work in the afternoons after the high school let out, since classes for the University of Kentucky branch were held in the high school building. Julie, Will, and I were left to ourselves. I had a fear that the communists would break through the Berlin Wall. There was a lot in the newspapers and on the news about the situation in Germany. While I got Julie ready for bed, Will watched television. I dreaded seeing the evening news but forced myself to watch. If nothing was mentioned to disturb me, I was relieved and enjoyed the rest of the evening. I especially liked Jack Paar's Tonight Show. Walter often went out drinking with friends after classes and came home late. Before going to sleep I could hear the sirens on the Dixie Highway and prayed Walter was not in a wreck. Fortunately, at that time his drinking did not interfere with his teaching.

Sometimes the children and I rode the bus to Richmond to spend a couple of nights with my parents on the farm. We were all happy to return. When Julie was just crawling I put her down at the front door to take off my coat, and she remembered that her toys were in the back of the house and headed for them. She had an enormous appetite. Occasionally, I would feed visiting children at a card table in the pantry. Julie finished her food and when the other children left the table she went around and cleaned up their plates. She didn't walk until she was fifteen months old, content to crawl to her little chair, climb up, and sit on it.

Will attended a play school, and another mother and I shared rides. Often I would ask the little friend to stay for the afternoon and play with Will. "Are you having hot dogs for lunch?" he would ask. I knew to be prepared, and later I would walk him home through the cemetery since his house was on the other side. I supplied flowers for our table from the wreaths in the cemetery, and Will learned to fish in the cemetery pond. He baited his own hook with bacon and pulled out little fish not much larger than minnows.

One of Walter's teaching fellows was Jack Heimer. We became good friends with him and his wife, Anne. Their children, Karen, Kim, and Larry, were about the ages of our children. On Sunday nights the dads kept the children and Anne and I would drive over the river to the movies in Cincinnati.

Both Julie and Will were baptized by the Episcopal minister while we lived in Erlanger. At the time Walter and I were
married, I was an active member of the Baptist Church, and
though Walter was not a member, he often spoke of his love
for his grandfather who was a Presbyterian minister. In Lexington, we were invited by his friend Evan Bullock to attend
his Episcopal church in Versailles. We took the children — baby
Julie and Will (four-years-old) to the services. Afterwards we
attended the coffee hour and sometimes went home with Evan
for Sunday dinner.

At that time little boys still needed dress shoes for church
and sneakers for play. One Saturday I took Will shoe shopping and he was thrilled to get two new pairs of shoes in one
day. He wanted to wear the sneakers to church, but I said they
were not appropriate and said he had to wear the dress shoes.
When we knelt for prayers, four sneaker clad feet came stick-
ing out under the seat in front of us. Will could hardly contain
himself, whispering "See, see," and pointing at the sneaker-
clad feet.

After we moved to Erlanger, both Walter and I, along
with another couple, took instruction from Father Willis to be
confirmed in the Episcopal Church. The classes were held in
our home on Sunday afternoons. I always put a roast in the
oven before leaving for church and invited Father Willis to
have lunch with us. When it came time for confirmation, Walter
said he didn't have the faith required for membership in the
church. Along with the other couple, I was confirmed when
the bishop came to Cold Spring. I was terribly disappointed
that we couldn't share the church experience as a family.

Many years later Walter was confirmed by Father William Black and became a member of the church in Athens, Ohio.
A few years later, Father Black read Walter's burial service
under a tree in the Richmond cemetery.

Jamie Tevis

Book Reviews for *The Hustler* Come In

Walter joined a clipping service and reviews of *The Hustler* came in from all over the United States:

> "The author of *The Hustler* writes
> like a streak, making straight pool as
> exciting as a Stanley Ketchell fight.
> This is a fine, swift, wanton, offbeat
> novel." (Rex Lardner in the *New
> York Times* January 25, 1959)

> "*The Hustler* opens the door on a
> world that books have not yet made
> commonplace...the crises are
> intense...a smoky, seedy world be-
> comes sharply alive . . . If
> Hemingway had the passion for
> pool that he had for bullfighting, his
> hero might have been Eddie
> Felson." (*Time*, January 12, 1959)

By the time school was out in the spring of 1959, Walter had decided he needed a Ph.D. if he was to continue teaching, so he chose the creative writing program at the University of Iowa in Iowa City, where he could use *The Hustler* as a dissertation. We decided to leave the house in Erlanger and travel until we were due in Iowa City in September. We traveled for several weeks through Canada. We set an easy pace, picnicked, fished, and stayed in cabins at night. The children soon adjusted to the routine. Will loved to fish. Julie was happy at mealtimes to eat a jar of cold baby food. One rainy Sunday night we rented a cabin with no grocery store open near by, and the supplies we carried with us were low. I prepared a meal of rice and butter to go with two or three small fish, and we went to bed full and content.

Iowa City, Iowa (Fall 1959-August 1960)

We arrived in Iowa City in the fall of 1959. Will was ready for kindergarten and Julie was almost two. We rented a big motel room with a kitchenette until we could find a house. Walter had inherited $6,000 from his Aunt Sallie, so we had money for a down payment on a house. We were shown several houses, including one that had been on the market for two years. The day we were to make our bid, someone came in from out of town and bought it. I was very disappointed. We bought our second choice, a nice two-story, white frame house on Court Street across from the Grant Wood house and near a school. The house we bought was a good one with wonderful neighbors, but whenever I passed the house that we almost bought, I wondered what life would have been like if I had gotten my wish.

Walter enrolled in the writing program, Will went to kindergarten with other neighborhood children, and Julie and I stayed home. The school was almost in the backyard and never closed for snow. If you could get there, you went. Buses and cars drove on the packed ice.

When it was snowing, the radio warned travelers to carry blankets, a shovel, and an object long enough to make a hole in the snow for ventilation. Travelers were also advised to tie something on the antenna so they could be found in a snowstorm. I thought this was an extreme caution until one day in March we went to Cedar Rapids to get Julie a table and chairs with Green Stamps. Coming home, just as we approached the bridge into Iowa City, the sky opened and snow fell in sheets. Visibility was almost zero, but with caution we made it the few blocks to home. When we returned from Cedar Rapids, Julie had a puzzled look on her face. "I didn't see the rabbits," she said. It took a moment until we realized that "Cedar Rapids" sounded like "see the rabbits" to her. Another time Walter was driving home from class in our little white Lark and had to abandon it and walk home. He wasn't certain where he had left it but later found it in a snowdrift a few blocks from our house.

Julie's appetite continued to be healthy. She would pull out the bottom cabinet drawer and stand on it to watch me prepare dinner and beg for a bite of whatever I was fixing. "One for Daddy," she would say. I would give her a bite of potato or carrot and she would run into the living room and hand it to Walter. "One for Will," she would say when she returned. Soon she learned to stand in the doorway and eat the bites herself.

"Nice" came on the train to visit us in November, and my parents in the fall, but at Christmas we felt very far from home. Christmas morning Julie had an earache, so I took her to the doctor while she held on to her new Raggedy Ann doll. Both children had been sick for awhile, and one sunny winter afternoon I decided to take them for a drive in the country. Road plows kept pushing the snow back until it was as high as the fences. Driving was like going through a tunnel. The car had a flat and another driver helped us. Winter was not over yet.

We had good neighbors, and since it was the era of "stay-at- home Moms," we often had coffee together. Rose and her children, Martha Rose and Gary Lee, lived across the street. On long summer evenings, while our husbands studied and the children played, we sat on her porch and drank coffee. John-John Kennedy was a newborn, and his first pictures were in magazines along with those of his sister, Carolyn, who was the same age as Julie. Will and Gary Lee were learning to ride bikes, and Will ran into a tree and smashed his nose. Our neighbor, a doctor, said Will should go to the hospital to get it straightened so it would not give him trouble later in life. One painful pinch at the emergency room fixed it.

We had left our cat in Kentucky, so I promised Will another one. It seemed kittens were difficult to find in the winter since cats breed in the warmer weather. I belonged to a book club and put out the word that we wanted a kitten. Someone offered us a half-grown black and white male. One morning there was a mewing at the door and Will, who was up before the rest of us, opened the door and let the cat in. It was not our cat, but an untamed one. It went wild–running upstairs, down the stairs, scratching anyone who approached it. Walter put socks on his hands and managed to pick the cat up and throw it outside.

The landscape in the summer was monotonous, with green acres of corn going on forever. In winter, the farm houses looked lonely in the white snow. I often thought of the pioneers who settled the plains and the lonely lives they must have led, living in dugouts. A friend told me the story of her parents who were on the way to homestead in North Dakota. They were traveling in a buggy filled with potatoes and grain with a cow tied behind. The young man had built a dugout earlier and had come back to South Dakota for his wife. A mouse got under the young bride's clothes and the husband said he couldn't stop long enough to let her remove it as a storm was approaching. They survived the winter, eating potatoes and bread and milk, and had a baby before spring. By the time I heard the story, the couple had acquired enough land to give each of their six children a tract of land, a house and barn, and machinery to run it. The houses in Iowa City were very close together. I suppose when folk moved into town from the vast plains they wanted close neighbors.

My depression lingered, especially at night before going to sleep. Gary Powers was shot down while flying over Russian territory and this added to my anxiety. One night, after talking with a graduate student's wife, I noticed when I went to bed that the fear had lifted. Years later I asked Walter why we didn't do something about my depression, and he said, "We didn't know how to go about it in those days."

Will enjoyed Captain Kangaroo and Mr. Rogers before

going to kindergarten in the afternoon. One day Captain Kangaroo gave a recipe for tuna casserole. Will wanted to make it so I sent him down the street to the little corner grocery with a list of ingredients. When he returned he said, "I decided I didn't need the olives." Another time, we tried to no avail to find a piece of coal to make a crystal garden . He got an ant farm for Christmas and we ordered the ants. Will enjoyed painting and went to a summer art class where he painted a big pink pig and entered it in the art show. He was not as successful in music, however. The kindergarten teacher told him to sing softly when they presented their music programs. He did, however, learn all the verses to "Que Será, Será," and when we were weary after a long trip, he would lead us in singing it. Another car ritual I remember is that Julie and Walter had a running contest. The first to see a Mail Pouch tobacco sign on a barn got five cents. Julie usually won.

We bought a barbecue grill with a rotisserie, and a couple of times a week we put on a chicken and played badminton while it cooked. Often other graduate students and their wives joined us. Corn was the best—fresh from the patch. One evening we were making our order, one or two ears each, when a long-legged pregnant girl ordered twelve. She buttered them up and stacked the cobs on her plate until she had eaten them all. Another afternoon Rose and I sent Will and Gary Lee to the store for corn and cooked up a pot for an afternoon snack.

During our stay in Iowa City, folk music became popular—Hootenanny, coffee houses, guitar playing, and singing at parties. Pete Seeger came through town, and his host tried to sell the cuttings from his razor. This was the kind of music I had grown up with, but I felt it more acceptable to listen to the Hit Parade. I pretended I wasn't enjoying listening when my dad tuned to "Grand Ole Opry" on Saturday nights.

There was always beer at the gatherings, but I never saw anyone getting drunk. However early in our stay, there was an incident that caused me concern. We had had a party the night before and a case of beer was left over. Next day, Walter was watching a Sunday afternoon ball game. He went to the refrigerator a couple of times for a beer and then brought the whole case into the living room by his chair and drank his way through it. At the time he had such a good mind that he could get by with drinking and doing school work. Even so, it began to cause me concern that his drinking was increasing.

Most of our experiences were pleasant, but Julie, at two and a half, ran into a little trouble. One afternoon she and a younger neighbor boy were throwing rocks out of a trailer parked in the alley. An old lady passed and they threw some at her. Julie was brought home by the boy's father who said, "Julie is a bad influence on our son. She is never to play with him again." I felt so bad for her that I took her to town and bought her an umbrella. Another time I took her shopping for a coat. While I was looking at the coats, she took my purse off my arm to get some money for the gum machine. When I opened the purse to pay for the coat, all the money was gone. We went home without a new coat, and I scrubbed the kitchen floor to work off my anger.

Walter didn't think a lot about the future, but he did want to write another book. Checks from short stories Walter had written while at the Highway Department dribbled in, covering our living expenses, and the money for *The Hustler* was promised. That winter of 1960, all the young writers in the Writers' Workshop dreamed of going to Europe to write. Ernest Hemingway was their idol. It seemed no one could write at home. Walter wanted to try an overseas trip to write a second novel, but I couldn't bear the thought of dragging the children into a strange country. One day, while driving home from church, it occurred to me that we could drive to Mexico rather than put the ocean between us and home. Walter liked the idea, and we began making plans to go to Mexico even though it interrupted his working on the Ph.D.

Walter got a leave from his studies, and we set out for Mexico with the manuscript for part of a novel, *The Man Who Fell to Earth*. (Walter called it *The Immigrant* then.) We rented out the house in Iowa City for $140 a month, loaded the green and white Chevrolet with clothing and the provisions we thought we would need for a year, and set out for some unknown destination in Mexico.

Will and Julie at a rest stop in the mountains of Mexico.

CHAPTER 2
MEXICO (AUGUST 1960- APRIL 1961)

We Depart for Mexico (August 1960)

We didn't have much money in the bank, but believed every day the first payment from the sale of *The Hustler* to the movies would come in the mail. We had rented our house, so we needed to leave even though the money hadn't come yet. The tires on our 1957 Chevrolet were not as good as we would have liked, but in the days before credit cards, we took a chance and left Iowa City in August 1960 with the little money that was left after purchasing the supplies we needed for the trip.

Walter could never wait for a trip to begin. He often had to go to a movie the night before a trip to ease his anxiety. We could have delayed our departure from Iowa City and held off the renter until the money came, but Walter's eagerness was both unstoppable and contagious.

I have often compared our hectic, unplanned trip to Mexico with the trip made by Martin Luschie, one of Walter's fellow students in the University of Iowa Writers' Workshop. Martin sent his family to his wife's mother, to fly in later to meet him in Mexico City. He found an apartment in advance. He knew where he was headed before he left for Mexico.

Unlike Martin, we just set out—destination unknown, somewhere in Mexico–a place almost as large as the United States. Sometimes Walter's gambles involved more than one person. Unlike Martin, we found our way to San Miguel Allende, which was the place for expatriate writers to live in Mexico.

It was exciting to be traveling, taking all our meals on the road, no schedule to follow, no deadlines to meet. I often thought of the Joads in a favorite book, *The Grapes of Wrath*, going across the country during the Great Depression with all their possessions in one old truck with bad tires. In a motel in Texas I asked Walter how much money we had. "Sixty dollars," he answered. We were not much better off than the Joads. Martin was renting an apartment in Mexico City, and we could make it to his place and call Walter's mother to send money.

Texas in August was even hotter than Iowa City. Riding in a non-air-conditioned car in August was similar to riding in an oven hot enough to bake biscuits. In a service station in Texas, a case of Coke was leaning on its stand. A Coke bottle burst, shattering glass and spewing its contents into the hot air. "That's the third one today," said the attendant. Walter filled the water bag that hung on the front of the car. I wet a towel in the bathroom to hang over the window for moisture and bought a large bottle of orange pop, and we drove on to Laredo.

Before crossing the border, we attempted to find a place for a picnic lunch from the provisions we carried with us. We got directions to a park, dry and barren as the desert. The only tree was a pitiful, leafless thing by an overflowing trash can covered with bees. I got out to pee in a can we carried for such purposes, passed around some food, and then we continued across the border into Mexico. Will, five, and Julie, two and a half, patiently rode on a baby mattress in the back seat supported by our bulging suitcases.

Walter, who seldom ran out of words, was silent. He must have been rethinking his decision to bring us to such a place in the hottest month of the year. I counted our blessings to myself: the car was still running, we had food to eat and pop to drink, and our health was holding. As we crossed the bridge into Mexico, I realized with a sinking feeling, my ability to speak the language was gone. A mile or two into the desert, a tire blew. Walter, fearful of heat stroke, got out moving like cold molasses. We all took a swig of the sticky orange pop to avoid dehydration and took the children a few feet away to stand under a leafless little bush. As Walter worked on the first tire he had ever changed in his life, trucks passed, each slowing down to offer assistance. Walter had the situation under control, so he waved them on. The generous gesture of help by strangers in a strange land cheered our hearts. It was a forerunner of the kindness we would experience many times from the Mexican people. Walter never found the hubcap. Another lesson we learned was that anything not tied down or locked would disappear.

An incident occurred along the way to remind us of how fortunate we Americans are. We stopped at a roadside stand for a rest and a bottle of pop. Soft drinks were five cents. A man and a little boy about Will's age were in the booth. There were some large sugar cookies on the counter and we asked for two. We sat down on a nearby bench and waited and waited. Finally, the little boy came running from their house with about half of a broken plate. He brought over the cookies on the best plate he had to offer his American customers.

Driving the curvy, narrow mountain roads with lots of switchbacks was hazardous but beautiful. High in the mountains were villages of the native Indians. We were following the Sanborn trip ticket, Sanborn being the insurance salesman for everyone driving into Mexico. He highly recommended that travelers stop at a motel kept by a nice lady, Mrs. Hollingsworth. We arrived about dinnertime. Will and Julie had been ace travelers, but Will was complaining of an earache. Mrs. Hollingsworth didn't give us the welcome Mr. Sanborn's description had led us to expect. She put us in a room on the traffic side of the motel where trucks let out their air brakes when they got to the bottom of the mountain. Trucks going up ground their gears as they shifted into their lowest gear. Will was in pain, and I lay awake most of the night worrying if our meager funds would get us to Mexico City.

In the morning Mrs. Hollingsworth was kind enough to refer us to a local village doctor, but she wouldn't sell me any of her ripe bananas for the day's drive. The doctor's office was full of Mexicans waiting to see the doctor, but he took us in immediately and charged a reasonable fee for some medication. We proceeded on through the mountains where there were lots of stalks of green bananas. The curvy drive made both children sick. Walter stopped to let them vomit and took their picture sitting on the rear of the car. It is one of the best pictures of our trip–Will and Julie looking very peaceful and happy high in the mountains with the fog behind them.

We took four weeks to travel from the border to Mexico City. We made our drives easy, took long rests in villages that captured our attention, and learned to deal with bouts of diarrhea.

Mexico might be fun.

Letters from Mexico

Going to the post office on the way to the market was the highlight of the day for Julie and me. Often the letters from home contained a stick of gum or a balloon for Julie, and her Grandmother Tevis sometimes put in a dress for her doll.

Our mothers saved the letters we wrote to them from Mexico and gave them to us when we returned. Forty-two years after they were written, I decided to take them out of the trunk in the basement. I took off the ribbon that held the bundle in place and read them. Reading the letters was like experiencing the trip again.

Jamie Tevis

c o Sr. Fidel Herrera

Apa 71

Linares, N.L., Mexico

August 27, 1960

Dear Folks,

Well somehow through the grace of the Lord we are actually here, 1600 miles south of Iowa City, sweating like pigs, and racing with ever increasing frequency for the bathroom in our first brush with what is humorously (if you can call it that) referred to as Montezuma's Revenge ⊬ the twenty-four hour trots (diarrhea, cramps, and general malaise for about a day or so; but not really very bad or serious). Through what I think is very good fortune we have found a place to stay for the next two weeks while we gather our scattered wits, acclimatize ourselves generally, and get used to this bewildering and a little frightening country. We are renting the very lovely hacienda of a rich Mexican, six miles north of the village of Linares, surrounded by a giant orange grove, in the heart of the major orange growing area in Mexico. The oranges are huge and delicious. Outside the house is a large, Spanish style, walled courtyard, ideal for the children (who love it) to play in. In the courtyard are several giant palms, a couple of dozen orange trees, some grapefruit trees, pomegranates, avocados (little black ones, not as good as ours), pecans, geraniums, cacti, and two nice, gentle dogs for the children. Beyond the courtyard is a swimming pool of concrete but too deep for Will to go in alone and pear trees. We have paid fifty dollars for all this for half a month, including all utilities plus a maid for all day once a week; and if we plan to stay, we can probably get a much cheaper rate. All this came about through the chance acquaintance, at a hotel in Montemorelos with an honest-to-God Texas millionaire who owns about five thousand acres next to this ranch (and apparently everything else around here) and who is a heavy reader with an almost servile respect for writers, none of whom he has met before. But maybe he has a plan up his sleeve, and wants me to write his biography or something. Anyway it's very nice, except for the climate. Incidentally, to help quiet your fears, we are only a hundred feet off an excellent paved highway that leads, after thirty miles, to a huge, well-equipped American hospital with many American doctors, run by, of all people, the Seventh-Day Adventists.

It's morning now and only pleasantly warm. It'll stay that way until about 2 in the afternoon, and then the sun comes down like the wrath of God, and you can't do much of anything (although the house, because of the trees, stays pretty cool by Mexican standards, that is). Then, precisely at 9 in the evening, a powerful, cooling wind begins to blow and it blows all night. It's cool enough that you have to pull the sheet over you.

This house is very nice. It has ugly, 1930's-style furniture, but the building itself is fine, with colorful tile floors, two big tile floored porches with Spanish balustrades and flowers, two complete tile bathrooms, plenty of rooms, four beds, two refrigerators, hot and cold pure, deep well water in great quantities, gas, electricity, closets, the whole thing. If we begin to make friends and become able to stand the climate, we'll undoubtedly stay here. But if not, if the afternoons are just too much for us, we'll go on south, up into the high-altitude plateau where most of the population of the country is, and look for a place, maybe in San Miguel or Oaxaca (find the map) or even in Mexico City. Up there the temperature stays in the seventies.

A feature of the country that should interest you is that the cucarachas fully live up to their reputation: they are very big and very plentiful. But, fortunately, they are not shiny and don't have those horrible long feelers and really don't shake you up like the smaller ones in the States. There are no mosquitoes or snakes where we are; but some grasshoppers that look like dragons and some giant butterflies (very pretty) and Jamie, bless her heart, found a scorpion in the silverware drawer. She almost had a fit. Now she can be seen at intervals with the DDT sprayer held before her like a flame thrower. (It was a tiny scorpion, and not poisonous.) But she has her compensations; the maid has just started doing our laundry.

We are completely away from the tourist part of the country here, and nobody speaks English; but we know enough Spanish to get by. The people are quiet, gentle (they handle children with an affection and grace that is very touching) and shy. The food is good, and cheap. Good filter cigs are a dime a pack; beer extremely good beer is a peso (8 cents) a bottle but they are little bottles.

The trip down was uneventful. The children took it well; the only bad thing was a flat tire on the desert. But I got it changed with much sweat but no hitches (while Will went in search of cactus berries) and all was well.

The Indian girl who works for us has been showing Will and Julie this morning how to make tortillas. They came to the house this noon proudly carrying hands full of grubby little, misshapen tortillas which they had made and which they promptly ate for lunch. When anyone says Gracias ℋ to Julie, she says, Por nada ℋ far more correctly than any of the rest of us.

The kids have no diarrhea, and possibly won't get it at all. They are having a big time of it. I think we'll be happy in Mexico.

Love from all of us,

Walter

80

Jamie Tevis

Rancho Reynoso
Hualahuises, N. L., Mexico
September 6, 1960

Dear Folks,

We are comfortable and generally pleased with Mexico. It is much cheaper to live down here. But we have not yet seen much of the country; we stopped here, near Linares, so that I could get in touch with Littauer and try to get from him the advance money that he is expecting from Harper's on my new novel, intending to receive the money here and then head south for Puebla or Oaxaca (both somewhat south of Mexico City) to take up permanent residence in the cooler high altitudes. But so far we've heard nothing from Littauer and I'm beginning to feel we pulled a boo-boo by coming down here without more money although we did have to get out of the house by the first of September, in order to rent it. We'll be getting a hundred forty a month regularly from the house and down here that should go pretty far which brings me to an embarrassing question (one which I suspect you have already anticipated); to wit, could you send money? But if not, could you personally lend me about five hundred? I would gladly pay all lost interest, handling charges and the like. I hate to ask, but we are low, and although there is a good deal coming to me in royalties and advances and I have two good stories up for sale I don't know what I would do for cash if one of the kids got sick or something like that. The thing to do would be to ask the bank about the best way to send money down here (probably a bank draft) and then air mail it to me, in care of American Express, Mexico City, and register it and all that jazz. But don't send anything here; we're leaving this address Friday and won't be back. If this is too much, don't worry about the money, I can probably borrow it from Littauer if I have to.

We won't stay here though because rents are high, and we need room for the children.

The climate is lovely, like spring the year round. It never gets over eighty here, or below forty. The children seem to love it. We took them to the big city zoo on Independence Day and they never enjoyed themselves more. Last night Martin kept Julie and we took Will to see a Zorro movie (*Zorro el Vengador*). U. S. movies are all in English, with Spanish subtitles At the ritziest theaters in town (some are as fancy as the Music Hall) the price cannot exceed 4 pesos (32 cents) by law.

During all this typing, Will has been sweating over a picture for you. He now wishes to speak; I'll take his dictation: This is a tyranno-saurus rex the tallest one, gray and the littlest one is a stegosaurus. You can't see so good but there are spikes on his tail. And he's red. He's a plant-eater and he has four sharp spikes to whap something with on his tail to make it go away. This is my present for you, Nice. ⨍

Bless you all, we love you,

walter

Jamie Tevis

Dear Folks,

We arrived in Mexico City before Martin, but we were able to rent a decent house on a cattle ranch with an orange orchard for two weeks while we waited for him. The house was large and clean except for scorpions in the kitchen drawers. I got "tourista" and broke our large bottle of Kaopectate on the tile floor. The heat was tremendous during the day, but every night at sundown a cool breeze blew in. A young Indian couple were the caretakers for the ranch. The lady showed Julie how to make little tortillas and to bake them over a grill heated by cow dung. Will and Walter swam in the orchard in a huge water tank with snakes. Thousands of yellow butterflies flew around the orange trees.

Besides a little cooking and reading there was not much to occupy our minds, and homesickness had plenty of time to take hold. On Sunday the rancher asked us to come into town and swim in his pool. His wife was a large black American woman who spoke English. I couldn't have been happier to have seen my own mother.

The ranch we were staying at was on the road we knew Martin would use to get to Mexico City. We put out a large, hand-lettered, cardboard sign that said "MARTIN" with an arrow pointing the way. He did stop a few days later. He spent the night with us, and before he left the next day, he invited us to stop off and stay with him in his apartment. We accepted and arranged to meet him at his place a few days later.

Warmly,

Jamie

Mexico: Early Adventures

We got to Mexico City about dusk when the traffic was dangerously heavy and no one obeyed traffic signs. It was every man for himself. Luckily, Martin knew the route we would be driving and was waiting for us in front of his apartment building. He had acquired a one-bedroom apartment in a high-rise apartment building so he could get started on his novel before his family joined him. We knew we couldn't sponge on him for long. Walter phoned his mother in Kentucky to explain that we were well but short on funds as the Actors Guild was on strike and there was no telling when he would be getting any money from the movie rights to *The Hustler*. Because of the poor condition of the phone lines he couldn't make her hear. He finally yelled, "Send money!"

We went to the zoo, and the traffic was terrible. We had to wait a long time to get across the street. I got so angry I threw my umbrella into the street.

Insurgentes Sur 300
Mexico D.F.
17 September 1960

Dear Folks,

First of all, you <u>cannot</u> sell a car in Mexico you can't even abandon one if wrecked. They won't let you cross the <u>border without</u> the car you entered with unless you pay a tax equal to the government's assessed valuation of the car. So we really had no resources short of selling the children except for you, dear, kind, rich Mother.

I got the letter and check a few hours ago, after one of the most agonizing waits of my existence. For the past two days all offices including the American Express have been tightly closed for the big fiesta of the 150th anniversary of Mexican Independence. It was only

84

this morning that I was able to go in a cab, with bated breath, to wait nervously in line, in order to get that gorgeous $300 check. We were down to less than a hundred dollars, too little to afford to leave the kind graces of our friend, Martin Luschie, from Iowa City, who has been putting us up for a week. Now that we have some money we are heading, tomorrow morning, for the little town of San Miguel de Allende with the intent of renting a house. It is a sort of artist's and writer's colony, and there is an American school there where we expect to enroll Will.

Mexico City is very fine, and I've been a little tempted to remain here. A lot like New York (five million people), it is amazingly cheap in some ways, expensive in others. A cab ride in new, better-than-New York cabs, with politer drivers runs from eight cents to twenty, with a four cent tip. Food and cigarettes and liquor are, surprisingly, cheaper than in the provincial town of Linares where we had been staying. For instance, beer is 5-1 2 cents a bottle rather than 8; cigs 5 cents a pack rather than 7; artichokes a nickel, pineapples a nickel, beef about twenty cents a pound (but it's lousy beef); bananas a nickel a pound; the best gin 90 cents a quart; fine wines 50 cents a quart. We buy at a big elegant supermarket that's as good as any in the States. Some things, strangely, are very high like olives and chickens. We had a miserable little, unpleasantly gamy and very tough chicken the other night, smaller than the average fryer, and it cost a dollar seventy-five. And eggs and butter are, though good, as expensive as at home (but we don't eat the butter for fear of undulant fever).

Love from all of us,

Walter

During our first days in Mexico City, I took the children to the park each day. Walter would help me across the street and return at an agreed time. One day I decided to have my black leather shoes shined by a man working in the park. I was sitting on a bench by a path where people were walking by and Will and Julie were playing on play equipment nearby. As people passed me they kept turning and looking back at me. I had seen other women get their shoes shined. I was decently dressed. Then I looked up a few feet away. Leaning against a tree, a man was exposing himself for my benefit. I was more furious with myself than with the man for letting him and the passing people think I was enjoying his display. The shoeshine man was finishing up the second shoe. Not yet knowing the value of the coins, I held out a handful for him to take what he wanted. I called the children and we went to the place where Walter was to meet us. He didn't show, and I was afraid to wait long for fear the man would think I was waiting for him. Carrying Julie and holding Will by the hand, we forged into the mass of taxies and cars that paid no attention to pedestrians. In fact, pedestrians have no rights in Mexico. If you are hit you are dead, and that is it. When we got back to the apartment where Walter and Martin were talking and drinking beer, they failed to see why I was so angry since we were safely back in Martin's apartment.

We stayed with Martin in Mexico City for a week until the money arrived from Walter's mother; then we moved out so that Martin could be alone to write. Since Will was ready for first grade, we gathered information about the school situation and decided to go to San Miguel where there was a Writers' Colony, an Art Institute, and an American grade school. On our arrival we found the American school was run by a lady who took the few American children who had books and let them advance at their own pace. Since it was expensive and our funds meager, we sent Will to the local Catholic school with a couple of other little American boys. We were able to find a decent house we could afford on Jesus Street around the corner from the town square.

We acquired a maid, as did all the Americans, who told

us it was our duty to give the local people employment. For $3 per week, Maria did the washing and cleaning. Each morning Will went to the Catholic school. Julie and I walked to the open market for the day's supply of fresh food and tortillas.

On the way home, Julie and I stopped for tea and a popsicle at the "Bug" (Bougainvillea). I asked an American, Sandy Cassatt (artist Mary Cassatt's nephew), how to ask in Spanish for a popsicle. He answered, "*Una palita, por favor.*" In the afternoon after naps, we returned for another cup of tea, another palita, and we met Will when he came by from school.

Jamie Tevis

Calle de Jesus 3
San Miguel de Allende, Gto. Mexico
21 September 1960

Dear Folks,

After some despair both over money until your $300 arrived and over the difficulties of living in hotels while searching out obscure houses for rent with an impossible language we have at long last found a home and moved in (last night, in fact). It's a big place, with two large living rooms somewhat sparsely furnished a smallish dining room, a good-sized kitchen-plus-pantry all downstairs and two large bedrooms and a small patio upstairs. The walls are white plaster (naturally) and the floors are all tiled. As is the case for all houses in this very old village, the front door opens directly on the two-foot-wide sidewalk; there is no door stoop, porch, yard or anything between you and the old women with baskets on their heads, the burros, the boys spinning tops, and the occasional cars. We are a block from the main plaza and surrounded by churches, the bells of which ring loudly at wildly odd intervals like every seven and a third minutes, or something and cobblestone streets. Also, tourists, since the town is a National Monument, an Arts Colony and all that jazz. But we don't see many of that type. We had hoped to get a house with a big central patio with geraniums and banana palms and all, as most of them have, but we couldn't find one cheap enough; other resident Americans have already grabbed up the best places. But ours has the advantages of a brand-new refrigerator (a rarity here), new and excellent mattress and box springs, location (right by the market and the square), and rent. We are currently paying forty-five a month; but I think if I promise to stay for several months I can get it down to forty, or even thirty-five. Oh yes, we have a new gas water heater (many fine houses heat with wood, even though gas is cheap) and an excellently practical sink (bigger houses have living-in maids and consequently more primitive kitchens). When we get a little money we'll brighten the place up with serapes and potted plants. Jamie suggested turning one living room into a kind of patio by filling it with potted palms and bougainvillea and flowers and all and I think we'll do it. Flowers are, of course, dirt cheap, as are pots.

The town is quite picturesque, but pretty dirty not filthy, just dirty and very old and very quiet. But it is full of beautiful little stores and shops, churches and parks. And when you walk down shabby little streets and happen to peer into some dilapidated doorways you see gorgeous patios, lovely furniture, and generally <u>very</u> expensive homes (by U. S. standards, anyway) even though it looks like you're in a slum. Incidentally, the most famous Mexican actor, cantinflas, has his home a few blocks from ours. Remember him in *Around the World in 80 Days* ⨍ ? We haven't seen him around and probably won't.

The best thing here is the climate, which is Honest-to-God perfect. Cool, sunny days in the eighties the year around and nights just cool enough to require one blanket on the bed or a sweater if you go out. There are nice beauty parlors, a movie (English language movies, Spanish subtitles, 16 cents admission) and a bullring. We haven't seen bullfights yet, but of course we will.

I hope I'll be able to pay you back the three hundred before long. After this letter I'll write to Littauer and then start praying for good news.

Write us.

Love from all of us,

walter

(Walter eventually did pay his Mother back when some money came in.)

Mexico: Hepatitis

People often said, "Mexican babies never cry," meaning, they were treated so well. One day an American couple was drinking tea in the "Bug" and their little girl, about Julie's age, was fussing up a storm. I whispered to the mother, "Mexican babies never cry." She laughed and we began a lasting friendship. Her name was Jackie Vilimas. She and her husband, Joe, and her little girl, Joanna, were from Chicago. They had saved up money to come to Mexico for the lively expatriate life. One afternoon in November we risked a trip on our bad tires and went to another town for a change of scene. We had red snapper for dinner. A few days later I prepared a Thanksgiving dinner for some other Americans and the Vilimases. The Vilimases did not come, so later that afternoon I went to see if something was wrong or if they had just forgotten. Joe held his head out the window when I, with a plate of leftover Thanksgiving dinner, knocked on their door. He said, "Put it in the refrigerator and come on up." He told me they had been ill all weekend, with Joanna, a healthy three-year old, jumping from bed to bed. I took Joanna home with me and contacted a doctor for them.

The doctor came in the late afternoon and said they had hepatitis. Walter came down with it the next day. We blamed the infection on the red snapper we ate on our trip. The children and I got gamma globulin shots right away, hoping to avoid getting sick. The procedure was to go to the drugstore for needles and the gamma globulin serum, then find the doctor, who was most likely playing dominoes at the cantina. Will had a light case. I knew Julie had contracted it when her stool was white. I knew I was sick the day I was writing Christmas cards and suddenly had no energy to go on. The disease is very debilitating and can damage the liver, especially if one is drinking. People who had it described it as feeling like "a glass with all the water poured out of it." Walter stopped drinking for a couple of weeks while he was too weak to get to the bar. He was lucky and recovered with no bad after effects. Jackie seemed to recover, but got chilled in the Chicago airport some weeks later when they were returning home and had a relapse. She was in bed for months. Jackie and Joe think I can do no wrong because I came to them when they were in need in a foreign land.

Wed., 23 November 1960

Dear Folks,

Just a note to tell you I'm better, even though my feet turned yellow last night. I'm sitting up, in bed, that is, practically all day now, eating a little, and yesterday, through help of an enema of blood-chilling force, that popped my eyes and made each individual hair stand on end like quills upon the fretful porcupine, I was able to pass something that felt more like civil war munitions than anything else. Anyway, it relieved me somewhat.

Jamie is at the doctor's now, getting gamma globulin shots for herself and the kids, and getting Will's pee analyzed he's been a little feverish lately, but with no other symptoms. As you can see, we are playing it all very close to our vests in a way of which I'm certain you'd be proud.

You asked a few weeks ago if we wanted to borrow more money. Well not yet our rent is paid and we have about 100 (1200 pesos) in the bank. This will go pretty far here; but of course I'm having unusual medical expenses. Still, what I'm saving on booze is not to be sneezed at (only wept over) so maybe we're breaking even on the hepatitis. Anyway, before we go broke I expect to get either 750 to 1000 from Harpers on the new book or the 10 G's from the movie.

Love from all of us,

Walter

December 5

Dear Folks,

Now that the Christmas season is here we think even more of home. Thank you for the money. The children have so little to play with that they appreciate any sort of toy. I think that if you mailed the children's little things first class or stuck the doll dress in an envelope we would not have to pay duty. We have some friends (both in bed with hepatitis) who get little packages from home first class and without duty. Don't bother to send money and Walter's packages. Christmas in June is fun also. Don't worry about them, whatever.

Today we are making Santas and Christmas trees and such. The little Mexican boy who empties our trash is helping Will, and Julie is helping everybody. Her latest is to be the second maid. I told her she was the prettiest maid I had and she said, "With brown eyes."

Will has a light case of hepatitis and has not been sick enough to stay in bed. I have tried to keep him in. I think Julie is getting it. Will is turning back to natural eye color and his temper is improving. This being out of school is no good. He refused to learn from me because he wants his Daddy to teach him and Walter has not felt like it. I read him many books that we get from the library which helps pass the time.

Today Walter is having a writer's meeting on the patio where they are discussing if he should sign the contract for *The Man Who Fell to Earth*. They have told him that he is lucky to get a good house like Harper's to publish a science fiction novel and he should take it.

It has been pleasant having Walter home and he is a good patient. I am not so good a listener at night after I have put in a full day and he is wakeful after a day in bed, but we enjoy the fire and the quiet hours after the children are in bed. We all like Mexico better after getting a nice house with a yard and patio.

The first day Walter went out he was so happy that he went to a bar and had a couple of drinks when he's not supposed to drink for at least a month and most doctors say not drink for a year. The doctors here don't know much about the disease so if you could find out the latest on hepatitis and what drinking will do to the liver I will be greatly relieved. Maybe it will not hurt him much and then it may hurt his health in years to come. There is great danger of a relapse but he is going slow. It is going to take him a long time to get his strength back.

Jamie Tevis

I enjoyed Thanksgiving because it was one time when I felt that I had done something for someone else. I cooked one of these lousy Mexican chickens and nine of us ate it. The pumpkin pie I made in a skillet. Our friends that I mentioned who have hepatitis and were too sick to raise their heads were glad to get anything to eat. We also shared with the trash boy and the maid. When the time came for me to eat there was nothing left but bone. Walter is very good to brag on my cooking but he says that I can't come close to you with dressing.

Love from all of us,

Jamie

14 December 1960

Dear Folks,

I am well, but with all the strength and agility of a three-toed tree sloth (or is it tree-toed three sloth). A rousing game of checkers would probably bring on a relapse. But I feel great. Jamie does have it; but, since she had gamma globulin shots a month back, we don't expect it to make her very sick. The kids expect it to make her very sick. The kids got over it without ever having to go to bed. Only dear old dads turned yellow, vomited in sundry directions, and made water like burnt umber.

You will cackle with delight to hear that I still cannot drink all this lovely cheap booze they have down here. You will smirk with pleasure when I tell you that I signed Harper's contract, like a craven hack, and will presently when the loot arrives send you about fifty dollars on account. On account I can't afford more just yet. And thank you, dear old white-haired Mother, for your quick and ready cash at low interest rate and no embarrassing questions asked. I'll get $450 this week from Harper's.

Love from all of us,

walter

Mexico: The Party Scene

Life for the expatriate community in San Miguel de Allende was one big party and lots of fun.

Most of the Americans in San Miguel had limited incomes that would not go far in the States but could provide a life of leisure with warm weather, a maid, a gardener, and cheap booze and cigarettes. There were two main ways that the Americans enjoyed these advantages.

There was a regular long-term group of retired people, artists, and writers who lived a disciplined lifestyle and didn't drink until cocktail time. There was also a group that got up late and went to the Cucaracha bar, "The Cuc," which was the setting for a kind of Alice B. Toklas salon, where they spent the night drinking and talking. This was where Walter spent his time with other American writers holding forth in the fashion of Hemingway and Fitzgerald. Later in life, when Walter gave a talk at AA meetings, he said, "That is where my drinking crossed the line and became serious drinking."

There were no TVs, no English radio programs, and no civic meetings to attend. It was the perfect climate for parties. There was one at a restaurant or in a private home almost every night. Since Walter was such a good conversationalist and something of a celebrity, we got many invitations.

All the Americans saw each other so often that we each felt the responsibility to contribute something to the evening, so any new song, joke, or story was appreciated. There were three of us with the group who didn't drink: Arturo; Joel, a writer; and me. But we found ways to contribute to the party atmosphere. Arturo was an older black man who had recently recorded songs from his childhood for the Library of Congress. Arturo and I often performed together. I played guitar while he sang.

The party to welcome in 1961 was a special one at the Ralo Restaurant. Jackie was too sick to attend the New Year's Eve party, so she let me wear the elegant black dress she had brought for special occasions.

At the stroke of midnight I was dancing with Arturo. I spotted Walter in a corner fascinating a circle of people with his brilliant wit.

Jamie Tevis

Mexico: Shopping

In the beginning, I tried to let Maria do the shopping and cooking. It was the custom for the maids to gather after the shopping and visit before returning to their duties. One day I tried to explain to her, in poor Spanish, that I wanted her to buy a two-pound soup bone at the market. She wasn't getting it, so I used my elbow and suddenly her face lit up. She came home with two pounds of elbow macaroni. We were out for the day and when we returned in the evening, she had prepared all the macaroni with tomatoes, enough to feed a family of twelve. After that, Maria did the cleaning and laundry. I did the shopping and cooking, mostly because I needed something to do.

Julie and I made a daily trip to the market. We leisurely (no one in Mexico hurries) walked by the grocery that brought in things like pea soup and sliced bread from the States at a premium price. Often there was a political parade with uniformed school children following along behind the local band–the same group of old men who played for the bullfights.

At one butcher shop that sold reliable cuts of meats, the butcher spoke English. I often stopped to ask him a question, such as, what did it mean when Will came home with the message, "Sister said not to come back." He explained that the unheated schools were too cool for the children–so just as Will was learning the language and beginning to read Spanish, his studies were interrupted.

A row of Mexican Indian ladies with shawls over their heads sold baskets of tortillas at the entrance of the large barn-size open market. The ladies were amused by the almost-three-year-old blond-headed girl who thoughtfully decided which lady we would buy her tortilla from this day, pointing at her chosen one. One time Julie and I got separated, and one of the ladies brought her to me.

The market sold clothing, household items, and plants,

and, best of all, there were many booths of fresh fruits and vegetables. On a typical day I might load my big shopping bag with dried beans that came rolled in a newspaper cone, a cantaloupe, green beans, lemons, potatoes, goat cheese, and one of the many shapes of pasta. I learned enough kitchen Spanish to bargain for our needs. One never paid the asking price, as the merchant enjoyed the bargaining process. For a few cents a boy would carry everything home.

The food available wasn't the same as in the States. The meat was cheap, but stringy. If I tried to make a cake, for unknown reasons it didn't taste the way it did at home. One time I bought what I thought were lemons to combine with evaporated milk for a pie filling to go in a graham cracker crust. The filling didn't thicken, so I added more lemon juice. The mixture got even thinner. They must not have been lemons. I have not seen the fruit anywhere since, so I have never found out what they were. Much of the conversation among the Americans was about how much they missed American food, especially McDonald's hamburgers. When we got back to the States, we found that they didn't taste as good as we had remembered. We discovered we had been homesick for the familiar.

Mexico: Pilgrimages

A few weeks after the big New Year's Eve dance, when the newness of the Mexican experiences wore off, I felt I had nothing to look forward to except to go to Brownsville, Texas, to renew our six-month visa in February. Depressed, I went to bed one day after lunch and pulled the cover over my head. Tiring of bed, I decided to get up and take Will and climb the Hill of the Three Crosses. People at the "Bug" often spoke of making a pilgrimage to it. I meant to do my own pilgrimage with a friend, but Will was not in school that day, so we went together.

Julie stayed with Walter, who was attempting to work on *The Man Who Fell to Earth*. Will and I started off across the road, through the park, and headed toward the hill with three crosses made of poles painted white that overlooked the little town. Soon we could see they were a lot farther than they looked. It was the dry season, and the walking was rough over the dry stubble of dead grass and weeds. We walked down into a ravine, up another hill, and down into another ravine. I could see that we could not continue such a route and decided to turn back, but I had lost our way. There was no path and I had no idea which way to return. Some goats were grazing on the hillsides and it was very quiet. We wandered around until I noticed a shack behind some leafless scrub bushes. We headed there and were met by a pack of lean, hungry dogs. Luckily, a very old, brown, wrinkled lady came out and called the dogs off. I used my meager Spanish to ask, "*Dónde está San Miguel? por favor.*" I knew that "*derecha*" meant left or right but I didn't know which. I gave her my hand and she led us over a little land bridge and pointed toward the town. Gratitude filled my heart. When we got back to the "Bug," people were going on about their business as usual or having their afternoon tea. Walter and Julie had hardly missed us and didn't seem concerned that we had been lost on a mountain. Thereafter, I had more appreciation for the local Indians when they brought cactus berries, pumpkin seeds, and sugar cane, and sat in the square to sell them for a few cents. We didn't make it to the crosses, but the shortened pilgrimage was a quick cure for depression.

There were a number of Americans with plenty of money looking for some way to spend their time while living in San Miguel. Besides Sandy Cassatt, there was Josh Reynolds, heir to the Reynolds Tobacco fortune. Next door to us, a friend, co-owner of Goldsmith Stationery in New York, and his Japanese mistress Cindy, moved in for a few weeks. Full of fun, Cindy danced in the hall with flowing scarves and played with Julie. One day, she climbed the fence that separated our houses and demanded the watermelon I had carried from the market for Julie's birthday. I explained to her that the market was some distance, and I didn't have time to go for another one, and I invited her to the party. She had to have it now, and I gave in. In a couple of days, her friend came and asked me to go visit Cindy. "She doesn't feel well," she said. When I went over, Cindy said, "When I feel depressed I try to kill myself and not bother anyone else." They soon returned to New York.

January 3, 1961

Dear Folks,

We are all well here but tired from all the holiday action. The kids had a big piñata on Christmas and we had a Chicago couple (Jackie and Joe) over for dinner. The week after that I finally got back to working fairly steadily on the novel, and we went out to several parties most notably a pleasant New Year's Eve party at the town's fanciest restaurant. Tonight we go to dinner at the Chicago couple's house; Friday night to a party at the Instituto the local college. So we are keeping pretty busy. But also being careful not to overdo, for fear of a hepatitis relapse.

Jamie and the kids recovered quickly from their short sieges of the disease, probably because of the gamma globulin shots they took as soon as I developed it.

The enclosed check is on account. On account of I haven't got any more, that is. By the way, I don't owe Uncle Charlie any money, do I? I mean, wasn't that original loan made by him to you, so to speak?

The weather is still lovely, and right now Jamie is outside, lying in the sun, while the kids are running around in the garden. The poinsettias are still in bloom there must be fifty large blooms on just one tree and so are the geraniums. But the weather gets cold enough at night to require a fire. Wood is relatively expensive, since there aren't many trees in Mexico. Also the reason, I suppose, why the paper is so frail and so generally poor.

Saturday afternoon I'm taking Will to see an amateur bullfight at the local plaza de toros. Our next door neighbor, a sometime writer named John Elbert, will be fighting calves with an ancient and bloodied practice cape given him by some local matador. Will can hardly wait. He admires John, who has been teaching him simple passes. John gets his cape and Will gets a red towel from the bathroom, and Julie, if she is feeling cooperative, holds her fingers alongside her head like horns and makes like a bull. So far, if she had been a real bull, Will would have been gored about fifty times. We've never yet been to a real bullfight; but Will and I have watched them a few times on T.V. from Mexico City.

We all send love. HAPPY NEW YEAR!

Love from all of us,

Walter

When I reread the Mexico letters, I was a little confused. We didn't have a TV. All I can figure is that Walter and Will watched the bullfights on a TV at the bar.

Mexico: School, Love, and Time To Go Home

The Catholic sisters were strict. They had the boys and girls line up in separate lines outside the door, and they called Will "Garimo," which meant "restless one," but he didn't complain about school because it gave him something to do. He came home for a two-hour lunch and practiced writing and reading in English. There was a small library in town where we often went for books that we would read in the evenings. We especially enjoyed B'rer Rabbit. Will was reading and doing quite well until he was sent home for winter break. He was in school again for a couple of months before we returned to the States.

One day Will asked for money for a package of Life Savers to take to a cute little Mexican girl, Ophelia, while they waited outside for the door to be opened. He came home ill and lay around the house all evening. It seemed that Ophelia was already taken by another of the little American boys. He didn't even care to play Old Maid with Julie, who thought she won if she got the Old Maid card. The next day he decided to take Julie to school with him. She wore her best dress, and Maria walked her to school along with Will. When the Sister saw Julie she got down in Will's face and said, "No hermana escuela." Julie and Maria soon returned.

One small boy came to our house as soon as we moved in and offered to take our trash for his chicken. In a couple of days he returned and sold us her egg. Will made friends with him, and they were free to run all over town, visiting shops and the market. One evening he wasn't home on time, and I was getting concerned. When he finally returned, Will told us that the boy's father had taken them on a trip into the country on a burro.

Maria and Julie (all the Mexicans called her Julia, pronounced "WHO-lia") had a routine. When Maria arrived in the morning, Julie would say in a pleading beggar's voice, "*Dulces*, Maria." Maria would say, "*Zapatos*, Julia," and Julie would run around looking for her shoes. Together, they went up the street to a cantina where Maria bought her a penny candy. All the Mexicans seemed to love a little blond-headed girl, but then they seemed to love all children. Julie requested a "sweep" for Christmas so she could help Maria with the housework. She was beginning to speak a little Spanish by the time we went home. On the way home, in the first restaurant we stopped at in Texas, Julie went up to a waitress and said, "*Carne*," meaning she wanted a hamburger. The waitresses laughed, and that was the last time Julie tried to use her Spanish.

April 3, 1961

Dear Folks,

Things are settling back to normal after a hectic week of Walter going to Mexico City, bringing Martin and his wife home with him, Easter, and getting income tax off this morning (almost normal). I am expecting a friend and her mother, who are visiting from the States, for coffee in half an hour.

We were relieved to find that the liver is all right except for the part that digests fats. Since alcohol turns to fat in the liver Walter is allowed just two drinks a week. The weeks are a little shorter now but he is not taking over one drink a day, which probably won't hurt him. The doctor gave him several tests and seemed to know his business, so I trust him, which is the first time I have had trust in a doctor in Mexico. Good thing he had a light case or he would have had trouble. From this point it looks like he can control the drinking. I hope he will not forget what he has learned here about alcohol.

The children were glad to get the cards. I hadn't thought of the Easter bunny until I read your card and then I rushed out to get eggs and baskets. No Easter eggs were to be found or food coloring to color the eggs, but I got baskets and some candy. Any candy is all right for Julie.

I took both children to the dentist for fluoride this week for four dollars apiece. Julie, who eats all the candy she can get her hands on, had one cavity and Will, who hardly touches sweets, had two more to add to the many fillings he has already.

I haven't had time to look about the silver jewelry this week but will do it in a few days. I am trying to get everything done so that if

Walter gets the book under way we can head for home. He is dying to see the movie of The Hustler being filmed but doesn't think he can finish the book in time. Our house will be vacant either June 2nd or 12th.

Will had to miss school today with a cold. Sounds worse than he is. Julie is getting so she tells us what to do. She says, "I am not going to take a nap." And she doesn't—much to my sorrow. I let her stay up with the maid and she comes to the bed six times in half an hour to tell me something. Walter got her a lovely doll in M. C. which she is so happy with. Has hair and is real cute. She hit Will with her old doll and tore the head off. W. got me a lovely wristwatch and I, too, am very happy. For Will he got a new shirt, which we all enjoyed. We are so tired of our clothes that we appreciate one of us having something new. Walter has two dress-up outfits and me the same and we have little interest in getting dressed for parties. We always look the same. I have an invitation to M.C. to stay with the friends from Iowa and do some shopping. I want some leather shoes and a bag especially. Clothes are as expensive here as in the States and not as good.

Time for guests.

Love from all of us,

Jamie

April 15, 1961

Dear Folks,

We've done it set a date for leaving. We'll clear out of San Miguel in two weeks, on Saturday the 29th. On the first we'll be in Laredo, Texas, will sell our car there (to a well-off fellow from San Miguel, who must cross the border with us to buy it, since a car can't be sold in Mexico by a gringo without a 100% tax) and then fly to Lexington, where we'll probably arrive the 2nd or 3rd of May.

Love from all of us,

Walter

Near the end of our stay in Mexico, some of the money from the sale of *The Hustler* to the movies finally came, so just before we went home we enjoyed a week in Puerto Vallarta, a seaport town. We flew in a small plane and landed on the edge of a cornfield. One week later, when we were returning home, we went to the new airport and were told the runway was not finished. "Come back later." We took a taxi back to town, had a nice lunch, and returned to the airfield. We left when the runway was finished and the plane was ready. To enjoy living in Mexico, one has to adjust to "*Mañana.*" After living there awhile, the biggest event of the day could be writing a letter or seeing the movie that came to town once a week with English subtitles. I hear that today Puerto Vallarta is a booming resort town complete with a mall.

Jamie Tevis

Reflections on Mexico

I had always had a great desire to play a musical instrument, and our stay in Mexico provided the opportunity. Leno, a young man who played in a mariachi band, agreed to come to the house and give me lessons. We went to the town square and chose a guitar from a peddler in town for the day. In a little blue book Leno drew lines of the strings and marked with dots where my fingers should go. Underneath in Spanish he wrote the words to the songs. Maria helped me with the words, which I had as much trouble learning as the guitar chords. I had plenty of time to practice, and before long I was singing folk songs at parties and returned to the States knowing the essential chords in several keys. It wasn't that I was a great performer, but since we Americans saw each other frequently at parties, everyone felt obligated to contribute to the entertainment. All the songs on the radio were in Spanish, and all we could understand was "*Coca Cola Grande–Hay Mucho Más*" (Large Coca Cola has lots more).

Maria, our maid, grew very fond of our family and we of her. The day we were packing to return to the States she was no help at all, sitting at the little table in the kitchen where she ate her meals with her head in her hands. I thought her toothache had returned. When I approached her, she burst into tears and hugged me so hard in her strong arms it took my breath away. "Julia, *Norte America*," meaning she would never see her again. My own mother never grieved so when I left home for the first time to go away to college.

Although happy to be returning home, I felt some sadness at leaving. I had come to appreciate the Mexican culture, the warm climate, the flowers, the music, the food, the bright colors, and most of all the Mexicans' love of life. There was always something going in the town square, especially on Sundays. We might go out one day, and ladies would be selling hollow colored eggs with little bits of paper in them. Children would buy a bag and smash them on each other's heads in observation of some festival day. Another day the trees in the square burst into bloom with huge paper flowers. Other times, for no obvious reason, a wooden scaffold would pop and whistle with fireworks. It was not uncommon to see a parade of school children or a political or funeral procession, the coffin carried on men's heads.

Even the Day of the Dead was lively. Street vendors sold little sugar candy figures to take to the graves. On another day there were cans of grass for sale. These were put together to make a lawn in front of an altar in homes at Easter. People were invited in to see Jesus in a coffin and be served a slimy green drink.

Groups of beggars rode the bus from town to town, and on their allowed day in San Miguel would yell, "*Señor, Señor,*" across the square if you hadn't given the expected peso. We got to know the beggars by name. One of the beggars was a woman everyone called "María." At one time she had been a woman of means, but she had been reduced to asking for handouts. She had a fur coat, perhaps a remnant of better days, and she wore it inside-out. I was told she did that to keep the children from picking off the fur.

One thinks of bullfights when one thinks of Mexico. The killing is only one part. It is a pageant with many parts, the best being the local band made up of men of all ages playing songs each step of the way. The meat is given to the poor if the bull is killed, and if the bull wins, he is turned out to pasture. Little boys spend hours perfecting the dramatic cape movement the "*varanica.*"

Will spent much time perfecting throwing a top, winding a string around it and throwing it on the pavement. He learned to crack a whip and could do the varanica. Children could buy fire crackers in the market and matches to light them. One day we were walking from the market, and just as we got in front of the police station, Will lighted one. It went off with

106

a bang. I kept on walking. I figured the police would not put a six-year-old boy in jail but might arrest the mother. When we came back to the States, Will never took the time to practice the whip, the cape, or top. American boys have other games that take other skills.

Mexico changed my life. I came to appreciate more than ever the importance of our family. We had shared experiences that brought us closer together. We found strength from knowing we could adjust to a different culture. At a family reunion when we got back to Kentucky, I sat the children on the floor against the wall and gave each a plate of food. People commented on how content the children were to eat anywhere they were put. Possessions came to mean less to me. I came to rely on my own inner strength. The guitar I learned to play in Mexico has provided years of pleasure and helped me make friends with people of all kinds who share an interest in music.

I doubt if Julie remembers much of anything from the experience, but she did study languages and has a degree in linguistics. I have fond memories of Julie in her pink nightgown with bunnies on it warming by the open fire while her daddy, night after night, repeated "Goldilocks and the Three Bears" before he returned to the "Cuc." On the count of three, she ran and jumped into bed for her goodnight kiss. I kept Will's school uniform — blue pants and maroon sweater — in a trunk for years. Although he survived his first four years in school, I wish his first school could have been easier for him.

Walter's goal was to go to Mexico and write a book or at least finish *The Man Who Fell to Earth*. He tried writing on the dining room table early on, but soon found it a lot more fun to go each day to the "Cuc" and talk about writing and literature with would-be writers. Days stretched into days and nights into nights, and a couple of weeks before coming home he decided he had better finish the book. The children and I left him the warm living room, and we busied ourselves in the

107

sun so he could have a quiet place to write. Walter hit me only once in his life, and I provoked it by saying, "If you had spent more time on the book, it would have been printed in hard-back and gotten the attention it deserved." I had hit below the belt. I don't think he would have hit me if he had been sober. Eventually, the book was made into a movie, but it never got the reviews *The Hustler* did.

I was homesick much of the time I was in Mexico. I counted that I drank 720 cups of tea at the "Bug," ate 300 torti-llas, and played 180 games of Scrabble with Delores, the next-door neighbor. Delores lived with John Albert, whose mother sent him monthly checks from Athens, Ohio. They were going to get married when Delores got around to making a wedding dress and tinting it with teas. Since she was not a virgin she couldn't marry in white. The noise of their fights coming through the wall kept us awake at night. John had written one book before he came to Mexico. He gave it to Walter to read, and in our moving about it got lost. I learned to make friends wherever they could be found, if not the kind one meets in Sunday school.

After we pulled out of San Miguel, it took us a week to drive to Kentucky for a visit with our parents, stopping in Texas long enough for Walter and the children to have measles in a cool, quiet motel. It was April, a much better month for travel-ing than our trip down in August. It took a while to adjust to the faster pace of the States and to get used to the taste of McDonald's hamburgers. We returned to Iowa City for the summer while Walter went back to graduate school. Will and Julie played with the neighborhood children, and I visited and drank coffee with Rose on her front porch across the street.

Mexico was a turning point in our lives. By Walter's own admission, he went from a daily drinker to alcoholic drinking. He got up late, had breakfast and lunch and went to the "Cuc" to be with friends who had similar interests and habits. Most had come to Mexico to write and ended up at the "Cuc" talking about writing. Each morning, Dennis, an expatriate who had been in San Miguel for years, could be seen waiting for the friendly bar owner to open the door.

Of course, there were the usual business people who ran the town, and most spoke some English. There were beggars who had their assigned day to work the town, and there were merchants who came in to sell their produce and wares at the market. There were Americans who were artists connected with the Instituto (Art School) and serious writers who lived a life separate from people like us who were in town for a few months. There were the tourists who came through for a day or two and had nothing to do with the society each group created for itself. Liquor and living expenses were cheap and all were in San Miguel to live an easy life.

The people who lived permanently in the town tried to follow the local customs, but those passing through didn't know customs such as not wearing shorts on the streets and not returning advances made by the local men. It is the Mexican male's custom to flirt. Our friends, Martin and Glena Luschi, came to visit us from Mexico City and brought a lady friend with them. While we were cleaning up after dinner, they were whispering about something Glena had done that made Martin angry. It seemed she had encouraged advances from a merchant when she was in his market.

After dinner Martin and Walter went to the bar, and we three women decided to go down the street a couple of blocks to an American-owned restaurant where there probably would be Americans to talk with. It so happened that this was a slow night, only one table of Americans — people I knew but was not especially friendly with. The man had a jealous wife.

There were three unfamiliar men hanging out in the dancing area where a mariachi band was playing. The best looking one asked Glena to dance and she did not hesitate to accept his offer. The second one asked her friend, and that left me sitting alone at the table. When the third one, a stout rough fellow, asked me, against my better judgment and not wanting to be a party pooper, I got onto the little dance floor. As soon as he put his arm around me I knew we were in trouble. However, I felt relatively safe as long as the other Americans were eating nearby.

Suddenly, I looked around and the couple was gone. "Come on, girls, let's get out of here," I said and got hold of Glena's arm. They were enjoying the dancing and didn't want to come. I pulled us along to where the others were getting into the van outside the door in the narrow street. The husband of the jealous wife had sized up the situation and didn't want any part of protecting three women against three big, tough-looking Mexican men. Uninvited, I pushed us into the van, and he drove us to my house. The men followed, shouting things like, "Come out here if you are men and defend your women's virtue."

The two women thought it was an interesting adventure, but Martin thought differently, especially since he had gotten his wife out of a similar situation before. Glena was a slow learner.

Walter's attitude was, "Jamie can take care of herself." I was glad to be behind locked doors and a walled courtyard that had broken bottles stuck in concrete at the top.

On Walter's birthday I invited our friends Rosemary and Arto to be our guests at a little party. Walter never showed, so we lit the candles and ate the cake without him. He said he had been drinking and talking with his friends at the "Cuc" and forgot. The next morning he was cheerful as if nothing had happened, which was his usual way of dealing with his misbehavior. We all went for a picnic and a swim at a resort-type place that had a naturally heated pool and showers. We came home feeling better, but such unspoken events left scars in the relationship. Walter's excessive drinking became a big secret in our little family. Since he had told me in the very beginning that he was not going to stop drinking, I always felt

I had no right to ask him to stop. I took on the role of enabler, running the house, caring for the children, and presenting us to the world as a happy family. It was a pattern we followed until the children left home.

I often said, "If I ever get home from Mexico I am never going back." Some old-timer would answer, "Yes, you will. Mexico gets into your blood." I did go back in the 80's, accompanying a group from a high school Spanish class. With the help of my hands, I could still use my small Spanish vocabulary, but I never saw our old friends, Leno or Maria.

I enjoy Mexican food and the spirited mariachi music. Sometimes I come across the little book Leno drew the guitar chords in, pick it up, and play through the songs he taught me. When I see a Mexican maid in a motel, I say, "*Buenos Días*," and think of Maria. I know they must miss their country and are always a little homesick. A Mexican friend here in Athens says, "I am always looking for someone with brown skin." Love for one's country has deep roots.

Walter on the movie set for "The Man Who Fell to Earth."

CHAPTER 3
YEARS OF JOY AND DESPERATION
(APRIL 1961- SUMMER 1977)

The Hustler Makes It to the Movie Screen

After we returned to Iowa, there was some mix-up in the Writers' Workshop over language requirements. Walter needed an extra year of a foreign language to qualify for the Ph.D., and he didn't want to spend another year in school, so he settled for a Master of Fine Arts degree. He graduated from the University of Iowa and began job hunting.

I think Walter missed the boat by not getting that Ph.D. His master's degrees limited him to the lower-level English and creative writing classes. He taught those classes well, but they were not challenging. Maybe the Ph.D. would have allowed him to teach more challenging classes.

Walter decided on Southern Connecticut State College, a small college on the edge of New Haven. It was a good choice and a great location. After two rented places, we bought a solid gray, two-story Dutch Colonial, walking distance from downtown New Haven.

We were living there when *The Hustler* came to the movie screen. A neighbor kept the children and we rode the train to New York for the opening night. The film was playing in a large theater and Walter reluctantly asked for free tickets from the manager, who was unimpressed that the author of the book the movie was based on would be in the audience. Tom Parish, Walter's high school friend from Richmond, met us at the theater.

We took seats a few rows from the front. I can only guess how it felt to Walter to see Fast Eddie (Paul Newman) and

Minnesota Fats (Jackie Gleason)–characters he had created–
on the screen speaking words he had written. I identified with
Charlie, the straight guy who kept track of the money and tried
to keep Eddie from losing it all on one game. (Toby Kavanaugh,
Walter's childhood, pool-playing friend, also claimed to be the
inspiration for Charlie.)

We waited through most of the credits to see Walter's
name come on the screen. Close to the end was "Based on *The
Hustler* by Walter Tevis" in small print. He vowed if he ever
had another book made into a movie his name would be in
large letters. We spent the night in Tom's apartment, sleeping
on a mattress on the floor, walked around New York in the
morning, and came back to New Haven on the one o'clock
train.

Julie, three-years-old, had been a baby when *The Hustler*
was sold to the movies. When we picked her up, she said, "I
didn't cry, but if you stayed away and didn't come home, I
would have cried all over the place, and I didn't need my soft
blanket you put in my suitcase." Will returned from school
happy because he had read from a chapter book for the first
time.

On the whole, Walter was pleased at the way the movie
followed his book and used much of his dialogue. He had no
idea he had created anything as important as *The Hustler*. If
only Walter's father had lived to share the success.

I think Walter would have liked to continue the excitement he was enjoying as a writer, but forces conspired to make
his writing stall out. His academic position took up much of
his time. He enjoyed teaching and did a good job at it. He chose
to be a teacher and a family man, putting his writing aside. He
made believe it didn't matter to him. It did. I'm sure he always
planned to quit teaching and return to writing someday. About
the time *The Hustler* was made into a movie, Walter finished
The Man Who Fell to Earth. After that, he wrote very little until
he stopped drinking and moved to New York in 1977.

Life in New Haven (Fall 1961-Fall 1965)

Our house in New Haven was a few blocks from downtown, near a good grade school in an older Jewish neighborhood, and there were two wonderful families in back. They welcomed a family with children and were delighted that we pulled open the curtains and painted the walls white, brightening up the place. They told us that a man had gassed himself in the basement with a hose from the water heater during the Great Depression.

As the furniture was being unloaded, Adrian, a little four-year-old girl, came through the fence and sat on the couch. Walter said, "Little girl, would your mother want you to be visiting strangers?" "You're not strangers. I know you now," she answered. Thereafter, she spent part of every day at our house. Julie was very shy and had not had a friend her age, so Adrian was just what she needed.

Her parents, Stanley and Marie Kulezky, and son Walter had escaped from the Ukraine just before World War II. They came to New Haven and eventually bought a thriving neighborhood grocery store. The cashier at the store was a man named Fred. Every Tuesday night Marie prepared dinner for Fred, for her friend Eileen, and for Julie. They were a godsend to Julie and helped her overcome her shyness. Fred took Julie and Adrian to kindergarten every afternoon and I went for them.

The neighbors over the back fence were the Kavanaughs–Tom, Madelyn, and their children, Tommy and Jamie. (The Connecticut Kavanaughs were no relation to Walter's childhood friends, the Kentucky Kavanaughs.) Soon after we moved, Madelyn called me to the fence that divided our yards and asked me if I could come over to be with her son Jamie when he got up from his nap. "I have been to the doctor and he says I am ready to deliver."

Jamie was about eighteen months, Tommy, six years, and now Michael joined them. We watched each other's children, shared birthday parties, and were in and out of each other's houses every day. When the children were in school, Madelyn often asked me for lunch. While I fed Michael in his high chair and pretended to steal sugar from behind his ear, Madelyn prepared the most delicious grilled cheese sandwich I have ever eaten.

Julie had her own ideas about sandwiches. We had a nice older lady who was the mother of a friend as a baby sitter. She had only one arm. After Julie observed her making a sandwich, she said to me, "Mrs. Richmond makes the best peanut butter and jelly sandwiches. Why don't you make them that way?"

"How does she make them?" I asked.

"She puts the bread under her arm and carries it to the toaster," was her reply.

We lived a lot of life in New Haven. The Cuban Missile Crisis happened while we lived there. I stocked a large closet in the basement with water, canned goods, flashlights, and blankets. The prospect of spending time in such a depressing place was not a cheerful thought. The children were told to stay within earshot of our bell and to come home immediately if they heard it. The worst part was when Walter Cronkite was on the evening news describing the Russian ships as they got closer to Cuba. We had guests for dinner, and I was so preoccupied that I barely prepared enough to feed us. Our mood was somber, to say the least. What a wonderful relief when the ships turned back.

Madelyn and I worked on sewing and art projects, the most memorable being covering shoes with satin to match party dresses Madelyn had designed by copying expensive ones she saw in designer magazines.

The next year, after we had moved to Athens, Ohio, we returned for a visit, and Michael took me to his balcony overlooking our former yard. "See. See. They cut down the tree." In our small backyard there had been one little pussy willow, but it was gone. I shared his concern and was happy to know he had fond memories of playing in our yard.

Will was the oldest of the children, and the Kavanaughs loved him. When Tom, their dad, came home they met him on the stairs. "Dad, here is Will. He's come to see us. Touch him." Neighbors like that are hard to leave. They were just what we needed at the time after the stresses of moving and settling into our New Haven home.

Keyhole Magazine Censorship Case

Walter was called as a witness for the State of Connecticut. The state was trying to prove that *Keyhole Magazine* — a tabloid — only appealed to the prurient interests of its readers and was not worthy of being sold in Connecticut. Walter, an English professor, was called to testify that indeed the magazine was of little, if any, literary merit.

One morning we overheard one of the New York lawyers in a phone booth discussing Walter. Soon the defendants brought *The Hustler* before the jury and proceeded to read some parts of it. The judge stopped the reading on the grounds that parts could not be taken out of context. The whole book would have to be read into the record. Connecticut won the case, and *Keyhole Magazine* could no longer be sold in the state.

The trial took place during the Christmas season and continued until the day before we were to have a holiday party for our friends, the Fitches, the Emmas, the Richmonds, and the Kavanaughs, as well as Adrian and her parents. I was so far behind in preparation that I had not a minute of extra time from arising in the morning until the guests arrived. Walter pitched in and ran errands. Being so far from home made Christmases a little sad. The children and I delivered poinsettias from the church to shut-ins with the help of Tommy Kavanaugh. Julie got a bicycle and Walter helped her learn to ride it. Will wanted a bionic woman, including all her internal organs, and he and Walter assembled her.

Summers, Friends, Drinking, Shows, and History

Walter never knew if he would have a summer school class while teaching at Southern Connecticut until registration. Even if enough students registered for a class, the college invested the funds allotted for salaries, and the investments did not come due until October. It was a long time from June to October. Walter always meant to use the time for writing but was never successful in producing anything publishable. The summers were often a time of tight belts with drinking but no vacations.

One summer I budgeted our funds, took the children on the train to visit our folks in Kentucky, bought groceries in bulk from K-Mart, made allowance for wine and cigarettes, and gave Will and Julie 10 cents a day for a treat at the local grocery. Each evening we packed our picnic dinner and headed for a fishing hole in the upper part of the state. It was a very pleasant summer. The next year, Walter had enough students for a class, but the summer was not as much fun as when we had more time than money.

We spent a lot of time at the home of Bernie and Sylvia Stoll. Bernie was a fellow teacher at Southern Connecticut who lived on a lake not far from New Haven. Their children were small, and once we kept their baby while they took a little vacation. That was our family vacation for that summer.

Poolrooms were becoming respectable, largely because of publicity surrounding *The Hustler*. Brunswick had more orders for pool tables than it could fill. Wards Department Store was carrying tables and products in the name of Minnesota Fats, who was going around the country bragging about how rich he had become after Tevis wrote that book about him. The covers of the tables changed from green to tan, and women and families were welcome in the new, brightly lighted places. Often after dinner, Bernie, Walter, and Will would go up the highway and play a few pool games while Sylvia and I cleaned up the dishes and watched the children.

Walter's drinking gradually got worse and worse. He had to drink more to have the same effect. He was staying out later, missing more meals, and being more verbally abusive in the evenings. He was verbally abusive only to me, never to the children, and always in the evening after he had been drinking. In the morning he behaved as if nothing had happened. Once when I complained about an especially bad time, he said, "If you don't like it, you can take Julie and go to your family on the farm. I'll keep Will." It was such a painful thought that I screamed and fell on the stairs. I would not even consider leaving Will. I decided to keep quiet when Walter complained about my cooking and to stay out of his way until he finally went to sleep. Raising the children and keeping the family together was my aim.

There were other excitements while we lived in New Haven. While making the beds one morning, I heard Jack Kennedy giving a speech at Yale on the radio. A few weeks later, on November 22, 1963, I was sewing upstairs when Madelyn called to say President Kennedy had been shot. Our friends, the Fitches, came and we watched the happenings on television for three days, carrying food to the living room to eat in front of the television set. I still remember what I served–chicken noodle soup and tuna fish sandwiches. Walter was watching when Jack Ruby shot Oswald.

A few days after Thanksgiving we visited with the Vilimases, our old friends from Mexico who had moved from Chicago to Boston. They took us on the Freedom Trail and to Walden Pond. I was very disappointed to learn that Thoreau didn't live totally alone for his stay in the woods. He went into town to eat dinner with his mother every Sunday night.

New York shows often opened at the Shubert Theater in New Haven. After watching the Kennedy funeral we attended a musical—a black spiritual—which was such a wonderful relief after so much grief. I don't remember the name of the show, but one of the spirituals was "Rise Up Shepherd and Follow."

During our stay in New Haven we saw many wonderful plays and musicals. I especially remember seeing *My Fair Lady*. I went to hear Peter, Paul, and Mary sing at the Yale Bowl, a few blocks from our house. We enjoyed a variety of restaurants, we had good friends, and we attended the Episcopal Church on the Green, where Will and I sang in the choir one summer. Walter went to see a counselor about his drinking, but when faced with the possibility of having to give up alcohol, he stopped keeping his appointments. Will was scheduled to go into the sixth grade in a rough inner city school, so when a job opportunity arose in Athens, Ohio, for Walter, I was very pleased to leave New Haven.

"Harvard on the Hocking" (Fall 1965-Spring 1977)

We came to live in Athens, Ohio, by accident. Athens, where Ohio University is located, was a halfway point between Kentucky and New Haven, and in the spring of 1965 we stopped over to spend the night with the John Jones family. John and Walter had been in graduate school together at the University of Kentucky. Our car broke down, and while we were waiting for repairs, John, who liked his job teaching in the English department, suggested Walter meet the chairman and apply for a position teaching creative writing. He was hired, and we moved from New Haven to Athens in the fall of 1965. "Harvard on the Hocking," as some people in Athens like to call Ohio University, welcomed Walter warmly. Later we learned of the interesting coincidence that Paul Newman (Eddie in *The Hustler*) had spent part of his college career at Ohio University.

Housing was very tight in Athens then because President Vernon Alden, a progressive president, was expanding the university and bringing in new faculty at a rapid rate. Walter traveled to Athens on the train ahead of us to find a house, and he was shown only three in our price range by the realtor. He offered the asking price on one that would do. A week after returning to New Haven from that trip to Athens, Walter and I were on Cape Cod, where he was teaching in a writers' workshop. I was standing outside the phone booth listening when Walter called to see if his bid had been accepted by the owner. Walter responded to the real estate lady's words, "What do you mean she won't take my bid? I offered her the asking price." "The widow lady says she doesn't know where she would go if she sold her house," the realtor answered. There was some more discussion, and they agreed that a house on Maplewood would be the next best thing. After we had lived in Athens for several years and replaced the leaky gas pipes, put heat upstairs, painted the walls white, and built an addition, I overheard an elderly lady in the grocery store say to her husband in a loud, stage whisper, "That's the lady who bought that house on Maplewood sight unseen."

We arrived in Athens a week before our furniture. We had planned to stay in a motel until it arrived, but after the first night we decided to make other plans. We had gotten one room for the four of us at the Athens Motel–one of those motels with a dozen or so rooms opening onto the parking lot.

Julie had acquired pin worms, and I took the opportunity to treat us all with medication previously purchased. Beds had to be changed every day, so motel living was a good opportunity to get rid of the pests. We slept comfortably until about 4 A.M., when I had to go to the bathroom. The door was locked, so I used the plastic trash can. About the time I got back to sleep, Walter tried the bathroom door, banging and shaking it until we were all awake. We got back to sleep and then Will and Julie, who had had a Coke before going to bed, decided they too had to use the toilet. At daybreak Walter went to the office for the key. "Oh, yes," the clerk said, "That door locks itself all the time." This gave us a taste of the slow pace of Athens compared with New Haven.

We went to Buckeye Mart, a discount store, and bought four air mattresses, and we enjoyed the comfort of our separate bedrooms in our new home, sleeping on the floor. I got stomach flu that I attributed to the water and spent a day on my mattress while Walter and the children explored the neighborhood.

We ate TV dinners sitting on the little back porch, legs dangling, and watching the birds feed on flowers in the backyard. We contacted a painter who never showed, so we set about doing the painting ourselves, covering the cabbage green wallpaper with oyster white paint. Walter went to Buckeye Mart every day for supplies, and the salesgirls always said, "You all come back." I told him they didn't really mean for him to return every day. The store did have a lovely view, though– from the checkout line you could see the beautiful green hills.

Athens at that time was a quiet place. The furniture came and the driver of the truck said, "I got to get back to New Haven. This silence is spooky."

The house was not the best, but the neighborhood was great. The grade school was across the street, and while I sat on the large front porch after dinner, reading and watching neighborhood children playing on the slides and swings, Julie practiced cat-walking the monkey bars. We were within walking distance from uptown Athens and the university, where I audited classes. The children had had to be attended when they played in the neighborhood in New Haven, but Athens felt safe, so Will could ride his bike anywhere he wished. Will was in the sixth grade and Julie in the third.

When Julie realized we were leaving New Haven close to her October birthday, she asked, "Who will come to my party?" I asked some people at the Episcopal church we attended for names of people with eight-year-old children. They found six little boys and girls who came after school for cake and ice cream.

Soon we were settled in and accepted as part of the English department family at Ohio University. The years under President Alden were exciting, with new faculty arriving each fall. There were few restaurants, so faculty wives gave large dinner parties. There were plenty of drinks and good conversation. We did our share of entertaining. Walter was a respected published writer and in demand for speaking engagements. We were close enough to our families in Kentucky that we could go home on holidays. The church was having something called "T groups," and we became involved. Going to someone's house after the meetings and going to retreats gave us the opportunity to get to know people in an intimate way. I taught Sunday school and helped with the annual bazaar. Our friends from New Haven, the Fitches, followed us to Athens the second year. We were invited to the Aldens' home to dine with Pearl Buck and Alex Haley, and we listened to President Eisenhower and President Nixon give speeches on the College Green.

We had good times together. Our tastes in movies were similar, and we always tried to see the first runs when they came out. We took the children to see *The Sound of Music*, bought the record, and learned the songs by heart. Some of the movies we enjoyed were *High Noon, Shane, On the Water-front, Bridge on the River Kwai, Bonnie and Clyde*, and *Deliverance*. I often stayed in the mood of the film and didn't care to talk as soon as it was over, but Walter wanted to analyze it immediately as we walked to the car. I saw *Midnight Cowboy* first with a lady friend and suggested that Walter see it. Since I had already seen it, I began talking as soon as we got outside. He had tears in his eyes and told me to be quiet.

Despite the fact that Walter saw double, he was an avid reader and would read anything in sight, even labels on cereal boxes. Each week he read the *New Yorker* and *Time*, sometimes calling my attention to articles he thought might interest me. Often he would suggest a book he had read. *The Fixer* by Bernard Malamud, *Rabbit Run* by John Updike, and *Deliverance* by James Dickey were some favorites we shared. He stayed up most of the night reading *In Cold Blood* by Truman Capote.

James Dickey came to give a reading of his book to the creative writing department, and we wives prepared a dinner for him and several of the writing students. He was fond of liquor and music. Having recently learned to play a few chords on the guitar in the Bluegrass style, he spent the evening entertaining himself. He found that I knew the words to "Your Cheatin' Heart," so he had me sing it, a couple of times. The third time he asked me to sing it I said, "Perhaps no one wants to hear it."

"I don't care what they want. Sing it anyway," was his reply.

We took family trips, and Walter and Will fished, built things, and remodeled a house we bought for a rental. Walter taught both Will and Julie to drive and helped them with their science fair projects. He played board games with them and taught Will to play chess. Occasionally Walter took Will to shoot pool. He was usually cheerful despite hangovers and a serious ulcer irritated by alcohol.

Walter was acutely aware that alcohol was affecting his

health and was sapping his creative energy, so he occasionally tried to stop drinking. His resolve never lasted more than two days. After a bad scene at night, I would approach him in the cold light of morning while he was having his soft-boiled egg and coffee and suggest he attend Alcoholics Anonymous. I had talked with Father Black, our minister, and he told me about the group that met in our church basement. "I will go tonight," he would promise.

At the end of the day, on the way home from his classes he would stop at the liquor store, buy his regular bottle of wine, drink half of it before dinner, and then take a nap just about the time dinner was ready. His excuse for not going to the AA meetings was that he didn't want his department chairman to know he had a drinking problem, and besides, he didn't like church basements.

I felt it very important that we ate dinner together. I tried to not respond to negative remarks about my cooking such as, "Why can't you cook potatoes until they are done?" as he pushed his fork into one on his plate with all his force. One time Julie asked, "Why don't you cook the potatoes long enough, Mother?" Looking back I can see I was a little rigid in my determination to hold the family together. I could not control the situation, but I could control the potatoes. If my anger welled up, rather than approaching a person who was not in a frame of mind to understand reason, I would sometimes take an empty wine bottle and throw it with all my might out the back door onto the patio and enjoy the sound of shattering green glass. In the calm of morning I would go out and sweep it up. The incidents would never be mentioned in the family.

Once when Walter's mother was visiting, he was especially annoyed with her and took it out on me by saying picky remarks at the dinner table. My anger got the best of me. I stood up at the end of our long table and aimed a glass of water at him. I never was a good ball player, and I missed him. The glass shattered, and water beaded up on the hardwood floor I had waxed the day before. I calmly walked through the living room, went upstairs, closed the door and began sewing on Julie's Easter outfit.

His mother cleaned up the mess and said to the children, "Your mother didn't mean it."

I did mean it. By throwing the glass I was saying to Walter, "I can't take one more minute of your abuse. If you are angry at your mother for things that happened years ago, and she can't do anything about now, say so and lay off me." I have learned since then that there are better ways of handling conflict, but at the time, throwing was the tool I used to release anger. There was a lot of anger I never released.

Years later, when Walter went to New York, he dug into his early life and his relationship with his mother. He did have a lot of scars, but I think she may have done the best she could at the time. During our married life I never heard him give her a cross word.

At night I often went out to community meetings, leaving the children to take care of themselves. The schoolyard was across the street, and Will practiced shots on the basketball court. Julie perfected walking the monkey bars. Walter read or watched TV with the children until the wine was gone. About the time I settled into bed with a book, I could hear the car pulling out of the driveway. He was going for another bottle of wine or to a bar. I prayed he would not get hurt, and especially that he would not hurt anyone else. He was never once arrested for drunk driving and never missed work.

I asked Walter why he didn't buy two bottles of wine when he came home from work, and his answer was, "I never intend to have more than a couple of drinks before dinner."

Once at a faculty party, he fell to the floor in front of his fellow professors, but still his excuse for not going to AA was the same. "I don't want my chairman to know I have a drinking problem." The truth was, there was a lot of drinking and lots of hanky panky in the kitchen at those faculty parties.

Some of the scenes are amusing when viewed from a distance. Walter seldom came to bed before 2 A.M., when the wine had given out and there was nothing else to do. One night he decided to try his hand at oil painting. He removed the pictures that hung behind the kitchen table and painted a Mount Rushmore-style picture of the four of us. As Will, Julie, and I came into the kitchen the next morning, we each gasped and said, "This painting has to go." Walter defended himself by saying he hadn't finished it, that it was just an outline, but he sheepishly went to the basement for a can of paint that matched the wall and covered it.

As the drinking progressed and the children got older and more mature, we three became the caregivers. Our house was not the place they brought their friends. I missed the kind of friendship we had had in New Haven with the Kavanaugh children and Adrian. In fairness, we didn't have close neighbors with children their ages, so Will and Julie went to the houses of their friends. Will was a second son to the Diles family and often stayed overnight with their son, Billy. Walter was not an abusive drinker, and Will and Julie learned to go around his moods. Will said, "I just had to wait for Dad and he would come around."

One of the sadnesses of my youth was that when there was a program at school, sometimes my parents would not be in the audience. For special events I would stay overnight with a friend since my parents weren't there to take me home. It is sad that I did the same to my children. On Friday nights, here in Athens, we often got invited to parties or had one ourselves, and I didn't realize then that we were neglecting to support Will at his basketball games. We did attend some Saturday games, but we didn't follow the games seriously during his junior high years. Neither of us was a sports fan, and it was not until I returned to teaching much later that I realized how important sports were to the whole family. When the doors opened for games, parents and supporters rushed in and filled the bleachers. Will did not go out for basketball in senior high school.

Often, Walter would feel guilty about not writing, and he would say, "Some writers produce their best works after fifty." As he approached fifty he got more and more unhappy. The sand in the hourglass was running out.

Pool Player Turned Into the Hustler

The success of *The Hustler* — the book and the movie — traveled before Walter. He was in demand as a speaker for faculty and civic groups and attended writing workshops as the featured speaker. The following article was written by his sister when he was speaker at a writers conference at Eastern University in Richmond. Betty had been a writer for a radio station in Cincinnati when Walter was in high school, and he had enjoyed riding the bus to visit her on weekends.

> "Pool Player Turned Into the Hus-
> tler" by Betty Tevis Balke
>
> (from the *Richmond Register.* 1967.)

> First literary success came to Walter
> Tevis, my brother , in a situation no
> editor would believe. He was grub-
> bing along on an emergency teach-
> ing certificate at Carlisle High
> School in Nicholas County and at-
> tempting–between teaching five
> classes in English a day, and coach-
> ing both the senior and junior plays–
> to write and peddle short stories
> mostly about pool players.

He was in debt (salary, he reports, was $1900 a year) and recently married and was desperately planning to abandon the literature business altogether when, to his amazement, *Esquire* magazine sent him a $350 check.

Meanwhile his love for teaching grows, to the place where it is competitive with the desire to write. I have never heard him in a classroom, but I am told he is an "exciting" lecturer.

He and his wife, Jamie, of Richmond, live in a rambling frame house in Athens with Will, thirteen, and Julie, ten. Jamie, with a degree in home economics from Eastern Kentucky University, is a good homemaker, but her interests have become, since graduation, more "cerebral." She plays a skillful folk guitar and sings, sometimes accompanied by Walter's monotone.

Accolades for his writing have been, of course, welcome to Walter. I remember him as a tall, awkward child and youth who was eclipsed by athletes and ignored by others up to the beginning of high school. Intellectual precocity, in those days, was out. "Now," he says, "when I walk around Lexington I sometimes see some of those high school football stars I once envied so awfully. They look pretty pedestrian now,

and sometimes they treat me with
deference.

Walter felt that his sister's article was a very honest one.
One thing we had learned from Walter's many interviews was
"never trust everything you read in the paper."

Betty's observation in the article is correct when she says
that Walter loved teaching. He was a very good teacher. She
was also correct in noticing the struggle between his teaching
and his writing.

University Professor

Each year the students at Ohio University evaluated their
professors. The four with the highest scores got $1000 and per-
mission to teach a class of their own designing. Walter bought
a fancy typewriter with the money, but I don't recall what class
he designed. It was a refreshing award after teaching the same
subjects year after year.

People who had him for a teacher, including the editor of
one of our local newspapers, *The Athens News*, still tell me they
learned a lot from his classes. I never heard him teach a class,
but I heard him at writers' workshops, and he was always entertaining. Professors were allowed to smoke in class, and
former students tell me he smoked and walked the floor, letting ashes build up on his cigarette, making them nervous.

Below are some reflections about Walter's teaching by
one of his former students, Clarence Page of *The Chicago Tribune*. When I contacted Mr. Page and told him I was wanting
comments from people who had been Walter's students, he
immediately e-mailed the following:

Dear. Mrs. Tevis,

How nice to hear from you.

Sure, I would be happy to share a memory or two of Walter, a man whom I found influential and inspirational, even if I was too thick-headed for him to turn me into a great fiction writer.

I felt fortunate to get into his creative writing class during my senior year (68-69), just ahead of a long waiting list of students who wanted to be taught by "The Man Who Wrote The Hustler," as Tevis was known around that enormous (15,000 students) campus.

We journalists in particular appreciated his gift for recreating the voices of ordinary working-class folks. He was also appreciated for the sensitivity and versatility he showed in "The Man Who Fell to Earth," then on its way to becoming a movie.

Anyway, the quote I remember the most from Mr. Tevis, as we students always called him, came on the last time I talked to him.

On a sunny spring day, at the end of the school year, I stopped by his office for a final visit before I graduated. With every contact with Walter Tevis I hoped I would hear the magic words that would turn me into a great novelist. I realize now that I was wishing for an easy-fix, shake-and-bake formula for success. Mr. Tevis's bright red hair and goatee glistened in that early summer sun.

I will always remember how cordial, patient, and encouraging he was, despite my inability, for all of his efforts, to come up with more than a few golden paragraphs, never quite a fully, completely golden story.

On that last day I took my last, desperate shot. I asked him point-blank for any parting words of advice. He looked at me with a bit of surprise in his big eyes. He grinned, shrugged, and said, "Well, Mr. Page, there's not much I can tell you except to get out there and live and love!"

I thanked him, although his advice disappointed me. He had given me no easy answer. Getting out there in the "real world," as we students called it, was a frightening proposition. There was the war. The draft. There were diseases. There were riots. More threatening were the hazards of ordinary life. Life was full of risks. So was love. Especially love.

Now, looking back, I realize that I came to Walter Tevis hoping he would tell me what I wanted to hear. Instead, he only told me what I needed to hear.

I will always be grateful to him for
that.

Thanks, Mrs. Tevis. I hope this
helps.

Cheers,

CP

Betty's article mentions Walter's monotone singing voice. It was remarkable; he just couldn't sing on key. We used to amuse our guests with three or four songs. Our repertoire included "You Are My Sunshine," "Irene," and "On Top of Old Smoky." Walter called off the lead in "Old Smoky" so everyone else could answer. We sang the answer-back song, "Four Nights Drunk," an old traditional song. We called it "The Drunkard's Special." Here's how we did the first verse:

Walter:
When I came home the other night
As drunk as I could be,
I saw a mule inside the stable, where my mule ought to be.
I said to my wife, my pretty little wife,
"Explain this thing to me.
How come a mule is in the stable where my mule ought to be?"

Jamie:
"You old fool, you crazy fool.
Can't you plainly see?
It's nothing but a milk cow my mother gave to me."

Walter:
"Well, I've traveled this world over
A million miles or more,
and a saddle and bridle on a milk cow I never did see before."

Poetry

Walter didn't write a lot of poems, but he enjoyed reading poetry. In an English class at Iowa he memorized poems and forever after quoted them around the house. I still hear his voice when I read them. These are excerpts from some of his favorites:

To His Coy Mistress

by Andrew Marvell

Had we but world enough and time

This coyness, lady, were no crime

We would sit down, and think
which way

To walk, and pass our long love's
day . . .

Let us roll all our strength and all

Our sweetness up into one ball,

And tear our pleasures with rough
strife,

Through the iron gates of life,

Thus, though we cannot make our
sun

Stand still, yet we will make him
run.

La Belle Dame Sons Merci

by John Keats

"O what can ail thee, knight-at-

134

arms,

Alone and palely loitering?

The sedge is wither'd from the lake,

And no birds sing . . .

"And this is why I sojourn here

Alone and palely loitering,

Though the sedge is wither'd from
the lake,

And no birds sing."

I remember when Walter explained to me that Keats died young of tuberculosis, and that both these poems speak of death and the need to live our lives while we have time. They seem a foreshadowing of Walter's own death at the rather young age of fifty-six.

Occasionally Walter wrote poems for me. I was unable to get permission from the Walter Tevis Trust to print them here. Copies of the poems are with Walter's papers at the Lilly Library at the University of Indiana.

For one anniversary he wrote me a poem called "After Sixteen Years." It recalled that when we met I was living in Carlisle at the home of Mrs. Cash—a widow lady who rented to single girls. I sometimes cooked a meal for Walter there. These are some lines I recall from that anniversary poem:

The way you stood at Mrs. Cash's
stove

Slicing potatoes into water, drove
into my head

something that keeps nipping at my
heels . . .

These dogs still nip me after sixteen
years.

Five years later he wrote me another anniversary poem called "December Twenty-Second." I still remember some of the words:

After twenty-one years

You should get a poem from your
husband

If your husband's a poet as he says
that he is . . .

You are stronger than gold,

Stronger than silk . . .

In my long and dumb life
You're the best thing there is.

Bread Cast on the Waters Returns

When Will was in middle school and Julie was in the fourth grade I decided that it would be a good experience for us as a family to sponsor a graduate student. We were put in touch with Tuan Van Pham, a 35 year-old student from Vietnam, by the university organization that matched students and host families. Tuan contacted us by phone, and Walter asked him if he needed a ride to our house. It was an easy walk, but it was raining. "No, thank you. I have umbrella," he responded. That was the beginning of our friendship for the time Tuan was a student at Ohio University. He was getting a degree in Industrial Arts, the only program open to him at the time. He understood his degree from the United States would not be very useful nor honored when he returned to the Republic of South Vietnam, but it was the only program he could get into.

Tuan missed his parents and six brothers and sister left behind so he came to our house often, always carrying a gift — a piece of jewelry, coins, a doll his family had sent for Julie, a native costume. Being very lonely, he decided he was ready to get married and asked his father to choose a wife for him and send her to Athens, Ohio. His father replied that he was unable to send a wife and told Tuan to choose a wife from among the Vietnamese students at Ohio University. He chose a pretty young girl, Hanh. They were married in our house by the Athens mayor as no Christian minister would marry them because of their Buddhist faith.

I made them a small, tiered wedding cake with a little bride and groom on top. Julie wore her pink costume with a good part of her legs showing as it was made for a small Vietnamese person. Hanh's eldest brother, his wife and daughter came from Washington, D.C., for the wedding. A few of their friends attended along with our family and, of course, the mayor. We received a warm letter from the father thanking us for our hospitality.

We helped furnish their apartment, which happened to be one street over, with odds and ends from our garage and basement. Soon they had to return to their communist wartorn country. We got one piece of mail from them with a letter and a picture of their little girl. A professor, who had been head of the Ohio University team in Vietnam, said Tuan and his family were probably put to death by the communists. We never heard from him after the collapse of Saigon on April 30, 1975.

Long lost friends return.
Tuan, Hanh, and Jamie in Athens.

Thirty years later there was a knock at my door on a Saturday, and there was Tuan, Hanh, and their thirty-year-old daughter, the little girl in the picture. She was finishing an internship in dentistry in Louisville, Kentucky. When I saw the familiar face, a little older but the same kind face I believed to be dead, we hugged and cried as we embraced. I invited them in and learned that they had lived under the communist regime for sixteen years while Tuan worked as a wedding photographer for a living until they were able to leave ten years ago and came to live in Virginia. He didn't write from Vietnam as he didn't want it known by the communist government that he had been educated in the United States.

When I told Julie and Will that Tuan and Hanh had returned they also had tears in their eyes. When he was visiting our home as a student, I asked him what he wrote home to his family that was unusual about us Americans. "The boldness of the children in the United States," he answered. I suppose it was difficult to be in a country where the children were the size of grown men in his country.

I had been going through some old scrapbooks the week before Tuan and his family appeared and came across the letter on thin, yellowing paper the father had written to us, thanking us for hosting the wedding in our home. It seemed it was a great honor that the mayor had come to our home to marry his son. Tuan's daughter, Anne, was especially glad to get the letter written by her grandfather. I gave them one of Walter's books, a book I had written, and a CD of my singing group. After they left I found pictures of the wedding and one of a group of Vietnamese students I had taken apple picking on a lovely fall afternoon. They had sung American folk songs that they knew better than most American students. I mailed the photos to Tuan. One of the Vietnamese students in the photo is very short, and Tuan refers to her as "the little girl" in a recent e-mail that I've included below.

I often passed the apartment Tuan and his wife enjoyed

for several months and always felt sad that they were probably dead. We are now in touch by e-mail, and my heart is warmed that our concern for each other has lasted for thirty years. He is 65 and I am 70. Will and Julie are middle-aged with families of their own. I thought the recent e-mail letter below bears witness to one of the good things we did together as a family, and it includes Tuan's memories of Walter. We tried to host other students, but none worked out.

Friday, April 27, 2001
Thank You for your Memories & Pictures
From: "Tuan Pham"
Dear Mrs. Jamie Tevis,

Thank you very much for your Memories and some old precious pictures that you have saved for 3 decades. Since our return to Vietnam, we always talk about Mr. Walter Tevis and you, hoping to meet him and you again. The "Miracle" came to us so that we could come back to the U.S. ten years ago, then last two weeks, we could see you and introduce to you our daughter. Your kindnesses and helps are always unforgettable. I still remember Mr. Walter Tevis as a "philosopher," with soft voice and gentle manners, he heard me talking more than he talked to me, and certainly he had been very helpful, especially he let me use his darkroom. I greatly regret that we could not meet him anymore but his gentleness always affects me. It was not appropriate to ask you about your private life, but when I read some pages of your book "Farther Along," I could understand something. You are certainly very courageous to maintain a small family and to go to graduate school. I will show some pictures you sent me to "the little girl" in one picture. She is in VA, not far from us. When you come to VA, we will invite her to meet you. We hope that some more months, our children will buy a house then we will invite you to visit us in Va. Always we are grateful to you, your whole family since Will and Julie had been so nice and helpful at that time. We wish you Good Health and Happiness. Sincerely yours,
Tuan & Hanh

I Reach for Independence/Alcohol Doesn't Do Its Magic Anymore

When Julie was in middle school and Will in high school, I decided to find work outside the home. To teach in Ohio I needed a course in Ohio history. Along with the required course, I attended workshops and classes in the Department of Home Economics to bring my rusty teaching certificate up to date. One day a call came from the director of the Manpower Program for adults in the vocational school in Nelsonville, about 15 miles from Athens. He had gotten my name from the college placement service. "When I heard your Southern accent, I knew you would fit the position for teaching Appalachian adults," he said. I was excited that I had landed a job after so many years as a housewife.

The job was gratifying, and I enjoyed every minute of it. Each person followed a course programmed to his needs. My job was to keep them on task. I had a wonderful boss, and the students were happy to be in the program, trying to improve themselves so they could get hired into the work force. Also, they got a stipend for attending. I had interesting stories to tell at the dinner table, and I got my first paycheck in years. It was the time of Neil Armstrong's walk on the moon.

One night in the summer of 1970, shortly after I had started my new job, Walter called from Jake's Bar and said he would not be home for dinner. We ate without him; I had made a rule for myself never to let Walter's late-night ramblings keep me from going to work. I knew he would be coming home drunk and wanting to keep me awake talking, so I went to bed in the outside studio.

About two in the morning, Walter came to the studio and told me he had tried to kill himself by taking an overdose of Librium. Then he passed out—falling onto the new bicycle he had given me for my birthday. I called the ambulance, and Dr. Larry Goldberg met us at the hospital.

141

"He doesn't need to be here. This hospital is for sick people. He needs to be on the hill." By "on the hill" Dr. Goldberg meant the Athens Mental Hospital. Walter was admitted to the hospital anyway. In the ambulance he had talked and talked. I was angry with him and didn't believe he had seriously tried to kill himself. It was just another case of his attention getting.

That night they put him in a room with an old man with cancer. Walter kept talking until finally the Librium put him to sleep.

I called Will to come for me, and about three in the morning we went to Ryan's Restaurant for hamburgers. It was a peaceful feeling to know Walter was taken care of, and we could go home for a few hours of undisturbed sleep. I would break my rule and call in sick in the morning.

About eight o'clock, my nurse friend, June, called and said, "Walter is awake and wants you to bring him a toothbrush." When I got to the hospital expecting to confront him with the possibility of going over to the mental hospital to discuss the suicide attempt with Dr. Harry Chovnick, Walter was so cheerful that I couldn't bring myself to approach the subject. I was drained—emotionally and physically. I lay on the bed beside him to get the energy to return home.

Walter once said before he quit drinking, "I fell in love early in life with chemical euphoria." Later he reported that "Alcohol didn't do its magic anymore." Walter began a long series of efforts to quit drinking.

At the end of the year, it was determined that the Manpower Program was not effective in getting people off welfare and into paying positions, so it was terminated.

Walter's sabbatical year approached, and plans were made for Julie and me to travel to London with him. We arranged for Will to stay with my friend June while he finished his senior year of high school.

I prepared for the trip with a heavy heart. My niece Gwen

was living with us at the time. Mealtimes were fun with the five of us around the table in the evening, sharing the events of the day. It was a bittersweet time because I knew the family would be breaking up. Will would be graduating from high school. Gwen would be finishing her degree and leaving Athens. Only Julie and I would be left to follow Walter for six months to a strange city.

As was our custom when driving to the airport in Columbus, we stopped in Lancaster at the Jolly Roger for donuts and coffee. A friend later said he saw us. "You were not happy travelers," he said. Will drove us to the airport that day and waved goodbye as we boarded the plane. My eyes were so full of tears I could hardly find my seat.

Walter was not in good shape. During the first part of our stay in England when we went out in the crowds, he would get cold sweats. Our outings were cut short, and we would have to return to our apartment. By the time he was feeling better, the public transportation had stopped going to the tourist sights for the winter season. We got a taxi to take us to Stonehenge from the train depot in the nearest town. It was a long trip, but worth the cost, and it was the most amazing attraction I saw in Europe. We discovered that many of the local townspeople had never made the day trip to see one of the mysteries of the world.

Of course there were the sights of London, but Julie, thirteen, was not the age to enjoy following her parents around London during the day, so we rented a car and toured some of the countryside. We drove to Land's End and especially enjoyed the Bed and Boards we stayed in along the way. One evening we drove several miles after dark and could not find a suitable place to spend the night. Rooms that were clean had a single light bulb in the ceiling and three beds in one bare room, not an inviting place to stop at five o'clock in the afternoon. Other places were above noisy pubs. Nearly out of hope of finding a decent place, we stopped at a house with a Bed and Board sign out front. The lady of the house invited us in and let us warm in her living room, the only heated room in the house. Three pairs of children's shoes were neatly placed against the wall.

The owner had just gotten her one extra bedroom ready to rent that day and was very happy to have Americans to be her first customers. She had furnished the beds with pink knit nylon sheets. Julie had a cot and Walter and I, a double bed. If we so much as moved a toe, the covers slipped and cold air rushed in. We spent the night holding on to each other and the covers and woke stiff in the morning.

For breakfast we were served oatmeal and bangers (sausage-like but stuffed with a grain). The voices of the little boys could be heard whispering in the kitchen. "WHO are those people, Momma?"

It warmed our hearts to be in real home with little children after being tourists for three months.

We were all impressed to be in Shakespeare's birthplace, Stratford-on-Avon. We visited Don and Jane Richter (friends from Athens who were staying in Arersham, a little town not far from London) and Duane Schneider, a teaching colleague from Ohio University. It was wonderful to be with friends from home.

Julie and I also attended night classes across the road from our apartment. I took a class that was supposed to review old movies. Usually the projector didn't work, and if it did, we had to stop everything in the middle of class and have tea—strong tea with lots of milk.

After our dinner, which usually included fresh cauliflower and lamb chops, we often played a British version of Monopoly and watched wonderful programs on television. We went to plays about one night a week—walking to the train stop and riding the underground subway. It was a long ride. We missed our car. In an attempt to limit his drinking, Walter would drink only after Julie and I were asleep.

Our visit to England was cut short after four months when Walter's mother died with lung cancer on December 19, 1971. Her death was especially hard for us because my dad had died a few months before we went to London.

Will picked us up at the Columbus airport, and as he drove us home we could see from horizon to horizon. It felt so warm and cozy to be back on familiar soil with the four of us together. They loved me even if my hair was green-streaked. Before leaving London, I had decided that I wanted to come home looking better than when I left, so I went to Harrods fashionable department store to get my hair frosted. A young man took sections of my hair, put solution on them, and rolled them up in foil for a certain amount of time. While we waited for the results, he described how he would dress the Queen, whom he considered to be a dowdy dresser, and how he would do her hair.

He was standing behind my chair when he opened the first section. I could feel his body stiffen, and he quickly re-rolled it. When he removed all the foil, I did not have a frosted blond look, but a green-streaked head of hair. It was an expensive experiment.

Back at home, I went to a beauty shop to get a haircut as soon as my hair had grown out enough. "Cut this green hair off my head," I told the beautician. I will never forget seeing an older woman going into the shop that day — with a sense of horror, I realized it was my own reflection.

I applied for a substitute teaching position, and finally, on the last day of school, I was called to teach home economics at Alexander High School. That day the principal told me he needed a permanent teacher in the home economics department for the next year. I'm sure he had read my résumé, which I had sent to him earlier, but it was Will who got me the position. The principal had positive memories of Will from a few years earlier when Will was in his social studies class at Athens High School. I was delighted to be offered a teaching position in a rural school where many of the students had backgrounds similar to mine.

Before school opened, I attended my first yearly teachers' conference in Columbus wearing a cotton dress and low-heeled shoes. When I saw the other teachers in their professional suits, I realized that I was just a housewife going back to work after twenty years, and changes were going to have to be made if I was going to feel professional.

While attending the conference, I took advantage of all the workshops, taking pages of notes and picking up a shopping bag of free materials from the display tables in the hall. I met the other teachers from the district with whom I would be working as advisor of the Future Homemakers of America.

My older, experienced department colleague gave me a ride back to Athens and insisted on carrying my suitcase to the car. I was relieved by this sign of acceptance since I had been told of a conflict between her and the person I was replacing. On the way back to Athens, we stopped for coffee at Frisch's restaurant in Lancaster where Walter and I had often stopped on our trips to Columbus. I remembered those earlier visits, sitting there bored and wishing I had a job. Now I had been hired and was scared. Was I qualified to hold a full time teaching job after so many years as a housewife?

I arranged to carpool the seven miles to school. The first day was given to teachers' meetings and arranging our rooms. I was introduced to the faculty and began to feel comfortable in the position. I was almost too busy to remember that Will would be leaving home the next day.

The insurance policy we bought for Will when he was a baby matured when he turned eighteen. It paid Will $1000, and for many months he had been planning a trip. He had decided he wanted to go "out west" and live the life of Robert Redford in the movie *Jeremiah Johnson*.

When I got home from school, Will was watching television. I remembered how I felt about leaving the farm for college, and I didn't want him to see how sad I was that he was leaving home. I rode my bike for miles in the hot, late afternoon. When I returned, I took a shower and the tears flowed with the water until I couldn't tell which was water and which was tears. We had our last real family dinner together, and I told him goodbye before I went to bed, knowing I would leave in the morning before he got up.

Will and I had always been best of friends. We had eaten breakfast together every morning from the days I prepared his Maypo cereal, before kindergarten, through high school while his dad slept and Julie prepared for school. We had always done many things together — making sculptures out of junk, throwing pots at the university ceramics department, gardening, and refinishing furniture. Teaching absorbed my mind, so I didn't worry about Will and trusted he could take care of himself.

Exercising his independence, Will didn't write except for a couple of times from somewhere in Colorado. Four months later he came home, smelling of wood smoke, with long blond hair and ragged clothes. To supplement his funds he had worked in a fast-food restaurant and lived some of the time in a tent in the snow with some boys who gave him a ride back to Ohio. He never talked about the experience, but the money was well spent. He has been content to spend the rest of his life in Athens County.

When he returned, Will worked at odd jobs for a while as a builder's assistant, roofer, and electrician. At our insistence, went to college for a couple of quarters. He enjoyed ceramics but not the academic courses that had to be taken for a degree. When he was 24, he married Lora Grueser, a high school friend of Julie's. We loaned him the down payment on a small farm a few miles from Athens.

One-on-One

For Walter and me, the rearing of the children had always been our common goal. With Will married, Julie in college, and me with a job, our lives changed. Through the years I had told myself that I would leave Walter when the children left home. We were not happy but neither of us knew what to do about it. Walter began to see his way clear to live another life if he could quit drinking.

Walter liked teaching, and he liked the sound of his own voice, but it wasn't enough for him. The creative writing classes didn't require research, so he had time to sit in the faculty lounge, drinking coffee and expounding on Shakespeare, Keats, and Shelley with professors who had Ph.D.'s in the fields. His department chairman did not push him to publish since he had two novels to his name, and he was promoted to full professor for the creative writing department. I did my share of entertaining for visiting poets and authors who came to give readings at the university. Walter was getting bored with reading the writing of students and felt more and more guilty that he was not producing his own work.

Walter could teach and drink but not write and drink. He struggled to control his drinking so he could write. Periods of days or weeks of sobriety interrupted his usual heavy drinking. To get back into writing, he attended sports events to see if he could write magazine stories about them. We went to dusty car races and to a world chess tournament in Las Vegas. Walter once said he really preferred the one-on-one competitions.

During Walter's last years at Ohio University, chess occupied his time. It didn't stop his drinking, but it kept him out of the bars. Once he was invited to play a computer match—man vs. machine. Man won.

Jamie Tevis

Chess with Walter

Don Richter was a fellow professor at Ohio University. He and Walter had known each other from the time we came to Athens but didn't discover their common interest, chess, until years later. Once discovered, chess brought them together several days a week.

I asked Don to write this piece for the book to provide a view of the hours and hours they spent at the game.

Chess with Walter

by Don Richter

"Hey, Walter, chess tonight?" It was seven in the evening and although we both had papers to grade, books to write, and lectures to prepare, the invariable reply would be, "Sure, come on over." I lived only a five-minute walk away, and by the time I arrived at the converted garage behind Walter's house, he would already be setting up the pieces or arranging his drink supply and my coffee. We would settle down to play game after game until sometimes two or three in the morning. For about five years in the late seventies, we played like this three or four nights a week. It became a nightly addiction for both of us. Now that I think about it, I doubt we played one game by day. Unlike truly serious players, we talked a lot while we played and I enjoyed hearing the details of his literary life, the writing of *The Hustler*, bitter memories of childhood illness, his agony of his persistent writer's block, his troubled marriage. An admitted genius, Walter played gambits with fierce abandon, sacrificing pieces for long-after advantage. Hair askew, thumb in mouth, Walter played with furrowed brow and always with a drink in his hand. One night we played at my house, which was not stocked with sufficient liquor, and we had to drive around to find an all-night source. Holding his liquor well, he played more intelligently with drink than most players sober. Like most players, we analyzed each game afterward, endlessly arguing over the wisdom of our respective attacks. We traveled to several tournaments together but never won significantly, our USCF ratings hovering in the high seventeen hundreds. In the later stages we played for a dollar a game and I doubt whether more than ten dollars changed hands permanently. When Walter moved to New York, I got back to grading papers and writing books. Still, whenever I pass the old converted garage, I remember with nostalgia those long chess evenings, but these nights Walter is playing somewhere else, thumb in mouth, drink in the other hand.

When I read this piece by Don, I remembered the callus that Walter had on the side of his thumb caused by his habit of biting there when he concentrated. The chess was kind of a relief for me. I could do my gardening or other evening activity. I knew where he was, and he was safe.

After Walter went to New York, he wrote *The Queen's Gambit*, combining his hospital and chess experiences.

New Strategies

Walter tried religion to help control the drinking, and he trained to be a lay reader in the Episcopal Church. He would go along with me on picnics and church events to get out of the house. Ray and Pat Fitch regularly exchanged Sunday night suppers with us.

Once, the church we attended had a weekend retreat at its conference center. We were in different groups for the classes, and the men and women slept in separate rooms. Walter had a chest cold and got up in the night to find his cough syrup and fell on the bed of the quietest little man in my group and knocked his bed down.

The second night he stayed up most of the night talking and entertaining an attractive female participant from my group. Not knowing that I was his wife, she came to our group the next morning all aglow telling us about the brilliant fellow she had spent most of the evening with. Walter and I got through the conference without a scene, but when we got in the car to come home, it was as if a curtain was pulled down between us — we had nothing to say to each other.

When we got home, I stood before him in the living room and said something must be done if there was any hope for our marriage. He meekly agreed. We got an appointment with Dr. Harry Chovnick, head of the local mental hospital, the only

doctor in town our insurance would approve. We had tried
other counselors, and they always competed with Walter's
brilliant mind to show that they were just as intelligent, or else
Walter would become speechless to hide his feelings. Dr.
Chovnick was even worse than the earlier counselors. We sat
in his large, impressive office in the mental hospital on the hill
while he and Walter verbally competed with each other. (Years
later, as Walter was returning from one of his New York visits, he said, "If Dr. Chovnick had been able to help us, we
wouldn't be like this today.")

One rainy night we were having a session in the mental
hospital, and Walter and the doctor were talking on and on as
if I was not in the room. Since I was in a place where crazy
things happened, I let out a scream. I probably would have
thrown something at the two of them if there had been something handy. I considered leaving and walking down the hill
but was concerned that patients as crazy as me would be on
the grounds.

The next words that Dr. Chovnick spoke were, "Walter, I
am going to put you in the hospital on Antabuse." Neither of
them spoke a word to me. We got in the car and drove home,
and never a word was said about my behavior. Again, denial
was a way of dealing with our problems.

Antabuse is a substance that makes a person very sick if
he or she mixes it with alcohol. Walter was in the hospital for
a few days to get the alcohol out of his system, and when he
was released he felt so good he decided to go to New York. In
the hotel he ordered a drink and slowly sipped it to see what
the results of the Antabuse would be. Nothing unusual happened — not the rapid heartbeat or red face he had been warned
about, so he got a taxi and went out for dinner. He ordered a
drink and a meal. He got sick and needed help to get back to
his hotel room. Antabuse seldom works to beat alcoholism.
The person has to have the will to quit drinking. Walter would
break up the pills and take a half, a fourth, an eighth...until

they were out of his system. We attempted to attend parties after he had been dry for awhile. I would be enjoying the party and look up and see Walter's face as red as a turkey gobbler's comb.

Dr. Chovnick also prescribed Librium to go along with the Antabuse. After he had weaned himself from the Antabuse, Walter had the month's supply of Librium filled and popped them when he wished, mixing them with alcohol. His AA group advised him not to do this as Librium could become addictive. I later learned that Librium plus alcohol had killed Paul Newman's son.

The days and sometimes weeks when Walter was sober, we had good times — doing home projects, going to the movies, or driving to Columbus for shopping and eating at a good restaurant. Unfortunately, staying sober was hard. He was especially uncomfortable at public events and concerts. He left Julie's high school graduation to go for a drink.

When Walter would restart drinking, I was very disappointed and angry. I always had hope that this time it was for real. One summer evening, I went outside in my nightgown to wait for Walter to settle down and go to bed. I thought of going to our long-time friend Reid's house but didn't think I was dressed appropriately to knock on his door. I kept walking around the block, and each time I passed the house I could see him still walking around in the bedroom. There was a beer can on the sidewalk, so I knocked it around the block with a stick. A couple was walking behind me, and when they passed I saw it was the elderly neighbors who lived behind our house. I don't suppose they had ever had a disagreement in their lives.

Our relationships with old friends changed. Walter had always been a popular guest at parties when he was drinking, but the invitations were few when he was sober. We drank cup after cup of decaf coffee at Ryan's Restaurant to help pass the evenings. Will was married, Julie was in college—the house was very empty. Our life together was grinding down like a pencil stub in an old grade school pencil sharpener.

Time To Get Sober

One afternoon in the fall of 1976 when I was cutting Walter's hair on the patio, I said, "I have tried everything I can to help you stop drinking. I give up. The pastor asked me to get you to his office using lies or any means to get you there. He has planned an intervention for you at 4 PM."

Walter willingly went to the meeting, and a date was set for him to check into a treatment center. He remained at the center for three weeks, and I visited him weekends. He was in bad shape; he had had delirium tremens. It was so pitiful—he begged me for the car keys so that he could go home for the weekend. I didn't give them to him as I felt it was the last chance for recovery. When he was dismissed, the therapists told him, "When you go home, do not make any major decisions until one year after your recovery—like a dog who crawls under the house to heal after a fight."

In his AA talks he described his first experience with alcohol:

> "I was seventeen and working during Christmas at Western Auto in Lexington–putting together bicycles. After closing on Christmas Eve, the crew had a party and I had my first drink. It went to my toes and warmed me all the way down. I decided that was the way I wanted to

feel as often as I could. I had heard it
took thirty-five years before alcohol
got the best of you. That was how
long it took me to get here."

At the same time Julie was preparing to leave home, Walter's crisis came to a head. When I should have been helping Julie prepare for college, I was making trips to Talbert Hall in Columbus because families were included in the treatment. At the end of his three-week stay, I went to bring him home and left Julie packing to go to college at Ohio University.

"Be out of the house when we return as your dad will be nervous about coming home. He has had a hard time at the hospital, having DT's when coming off the pills and alcohol. Get your boyfriend to move you," I told her before I left.

We came into the darkened house. Julie was sitting on the stairs in her bathrobe, crying, boxes stacked around her with the living room shades drawn. I figured she must have had a fight with her boyfriend, but there was no time to get into that. Walter was nervous about beginning a life of sobriety and especially about the liquor that was in the house. He requested it be removed. Julie got dressed and took it across the street to our neighbors, the Hollows. I told her to ask them to come stay with Walter so I could take her to school.

We loaded her things into the car to drive the mile or so to her dorm. On the way she popped her gum until I thought I couldn't stand it, but I held my tongue, knowing she was having a difficult time leaving home. Our home had often been a place of turmoil and tension, but it was the only home she had known.

To make matters worse, she had a boyfriend who told her she shouldn't contact us for a while and live as if she had gone away to college. He had problems worse than her dad. Since Julie didn't come home, I would meet her for lunch at Woolworth's on Saturdays. When she tried to break with the boyfriend, he stalked her. She decided to go to her dad's office to get help with the situation. Walter, Julie, and the boyfriend went to Campus Ministry to see a counselor, and the boyfriend agreed to leave her alone.

Not long after that, an even bigger problem came up for Julie. At one of our lunch meetings, she told me she was having a problem and needed to go to a doctor. I took her to see Dr. Kroner for a Pap test. We got the test results when Dr. Kroner happened to meet Walter at the Roller Bowl, where he and Will were playing pool. The Pap test was a three, and Julie needed to see him immediately. I had always told Will and Julie that if money could fix something, it was not a problem — Julie had a real problem. She went immediately to O'Bleness Hospital for a DNC. To our joy, the results were negative.

Years later I told Julie that the biggest crisis in our family had been when we thought she had cancer and could never have children if she did live. She was surprised. "Really?" she said.

Writing Again

As he became sober, Walter's mind cleared, and he was working on a new book, *Mockingbird*. Now he needed a new agent.

When Walter began writing in the 50's, his agent, Kenneth Littauer, was like a father figure to him. He could not pass the mailbox hours after mail time, just in case he had missed a letter. We went to Mr. Littauer's office in New York and he took us to lunch. He was a serious neat little man who told me right off he didn't want to see any pictures of our children.

When we lived in New Haven, I would suggest Walter take the train and go to New York to meet his agent, even if he was not writing. I suppose Walter felt guilty for having nothing to show him after he had been so encouraging in the beginning. He never once made the trip. Years later, he was shocked and saddened to discover that Mr. Littauer had died.

Walter asked his writing colleagues at Ohio University for suggestions about finding an agent. After he had finished enough of *Mockingbird*, he followed their recommendations and sent the manuscript to Bob Mills. Eleanora Walker, Bob Mill's secretary, began corresponding with Walter, encouraging him to continue working on the book.

In February, a handwritten letter came from Eleanora in Bob Mill's office. Walter always asked me to open such letters before I called him to tell him if the news was good. The letter was encouraging as I recall, more tantalizing than business, and in the upper right corner was a little heart colored in red with a marking pencil. When he got home, I asked him what that meant. He said, "Oh, nothing."

The sender of the little red heart may have thought it of little importance, but she didn't know how Walter was affected by little drawings. Recall the note I sent him when our courtship first began, thanking him for the big red apple? Later, he told me it carried lots of meaning and he couldn't get it from my hands fast enough.

The letter did not contain an outright offer to come to New York, be a writer and live the exciting city life, but from that point on, Walter began planning in his mind to do just that. His life with me became very secretive. His year of sobriety was coming to an end, his creative juices were flowing, and he could dream of a new way of life. A little help from his agent's office was just what he needed to start planning a new future.

The Man Who Fell to Earth Opens in the Movies

Walter and I had just returned from a few weeks in Europe in 1976 when he was notified that the movie of *The Man Who Fell To Earth* was opening in New York. Our funds were low, but I told Walter we should go as such events didn't happen every day. Julie went with us. Madelyn Kavanaugh (our friend from New Haven), Walter's nephew Henry Balke, and Eleanora met us at the theatre. Eleanora had seats reserved for us in a small arts theatre. The audience was mostly David Bowie fans.

The movie had none of the glamour that *The Hustler* had when we attended that huge New York theatre many years before. Walter was very nervous and said he would give the movie a "B." Still, it was exciting to be in New York and to see the movie that had taken 15 years to get from a book written in Mexico to the big screen.

Walter said in an interview in the *New Haven Register* in 1965: "The second novel, *The Man Who Fell to Earth*, didn't go so well. It's a rare one that does. It was a science fiction book published by a paperback company. I only made about $4,000 from it. I guess it sold about 300,000 copies ($3.50 each)–not bad, but not that good by pocket book standards."

The novel was runner-up in the Little Green Man Award for the best science fiction novel of 1963. Kurt Vonnegut Jr. was given the award for his *Cat's Cradle*.

CHAPTER 4
WE LIVE APART (SUMMER 1977- AUGUST 8, 1984)

Separation

At the end of the 1977 school year, Walter left to be near his agent, Bob Mills, and to finish the book, *Mockingbird*. I like to think Walter had the strength and the honesty to make it in New York, but I don't believe that was the way it was. He had talked for some time about taking a year's leave from teaching and going somewhere on his own to write. I was not against the idea as I didn't want to leave my teaching position at Alexander High School. Together, we had gone as far as we could go. Ever since his boyhood summer visit with his Aunt Myra, he had longed to live the New York life.

As time had approached for him to leave, we had finally said to each other many of the things we had been fearful of saying. The air had been cleared, and we were more comfortable with each other than we had been in a long time. The year after his treatment at Talbert Hall had been a quiet one. Walter was writing again and the book seemed to be going well. It was the year of the heavy snow when the schools were closed for weeks. We often walked uptown through the snow for lunch. Our last months together were a bittersweet time.

It was not easy for Walter to cut his dependency on his non-demanding job of teaching at Ohio University, drop his retirement program, leave the security of home, and face the most frightening question: "Can I still write? Do I have more books in me, or have I written my best material?" It was a big gamble.

Julie drove him to the airport before she left to spend the summer with her Spanish class in Mexico. Walter wrote us that he was living in an apartment near a card shop, and he often chose a pretty card to send to Julie or me.

In one note he wrote about his apartment with a skylight and about how he had put new locks on the doors. That reminded me that the last time we had been in New York together I had been frightened more than once and had felt very unsafe.

A couple of years before, Walter and I had been walking down Broadway on the way to a play on a warm summer evening. The sidewalk was full of people walking fast in our direction. A seedy-looking young man in a Navy cap and a winter coat came walking from the other direction mumbling loudly to himself. When he got to me, he turned and started walking beside me and raging obscenities into my ear. I pushed Walter into one of those brightly lighted shops that sell cheap watches and glittering things. I realized that the owner was not going to do anything to protect some out-of-town person who had gotten herself picked out of the crowd. I suppose I had looked at the young man, and that was why he had chosen me to harass. Luckily he went on his way.

There were other upsetting experiences. The street outside our hotel room was lined with young girls standing around in scanty costumes and painted faces waiting to be picked up for the evening. Drunks lay in doorways, so I had Walter walk as close to the curb as we could. Once we were riding a bus when a rough-looking gang got on. We got off at a coffee shop, and they all got off with us.

Walter had never admitted that he was afraid during that trip, but when he moved to New York, he found a neighborhood to live in that was much safer than where we had stayed that last visit.

In Walter's cards from New York he described how he was taking care of himself. He confessed that the omelets he had prepared for Julie and me were practice for leaving home. He had wanted to see if he could take care of himself before he left. In the months before he went to New York, he would whip up an omelet, using half the equipment in the kitchen, and nervously put it before us. Standing over us he would say, "How does it taste?" We would answer, "We don't know. It's too hot to eat." Before we could taste, he would ask again.

Another way he prepared himself for leaving was to take over the family wash. He ruined some of my favorite clothes. Once he bleached a favorite pair of blue denim pants with embroidery down the legs so that they never again matched the jacket. When he wrote that he was having his shirts done by the laundry, I was amused, but not surprised. He always loved shirts.

Here in Athens he had slept until ten and then called downstairs for me to start a soft-boiled egg and coffee. In one letter he wrote about his New York routine; he said he got up early, took a shower, fixed his breakfast, and went to the typewriter. He said it was better than being drunk and suicidal, getting up and starting the day with a hangover and a guilty conscience.

During the summer he wrote that he thought some of what he was doing was sheer fantasy. His letter noted that he was still under contract with Ohio University for the coming year, and the time was getting near when he would have to decide if he was returning or breaking his contract. He said it troubled him that he second-guessed his ability to write a good book while finishing one that his agent said was good. He also felt bad about second-guessing the decision to live in New York even though he had dreamed of living there all his life. He said he second-guessed leaving me too, even though he had dreamed of doing that for years. While in this mood, he returned home three or four times as he wrestled with the decision to take the big gamble or not. Each time he came back to Athens he came back "to stay," but he always returned to New York.

One of his strong ties to New York was his psychotherapist, Harry. When the pain of his past and of his behavior got too painful to deal with, he fled. He wrote that Harry was helping him face several issues: the pain of being left behind in California, the reasons he needed to be away from his family to write, the influence his mother had had on his life, and his feelings for his father. Walter's letters got farther apart, but I could tell that he was struggling with these issues.

The last time he came home, I left in the morning for school thinking he had decided to remain in Athens and teach at the university. He called me from my classroom in the mid-morning saying he had decided to return to New York. When I got home, I found a note on my pillow saying he would always care for me. I was relieved that he had made a decision. It had been a painful, confusing time while he was making up his mind.

That fall Walter took a leave of absence for one year and then cut his ties with the university. He placed his bet on his writing, and he never returned to teaching. In 1980, soon after going to New York, *Mockingbird* was accepted for publication, and the advance gave Walter the money he needed to live there. He had a book of short stories, *Far From Home*, published the next year. A book based on his childhood hospital experience, *Queens Gambit*, followed in 1983. In those same three years, he also had several magazine stories published. He had said his goal was to stay sober and to write one book a year. He succeeded with the first goal and almost did with the second.

Walter's letters before and after that final separation made it seem that he was living alone. He talked of not seeing anyone he knew for days at a time. He kept it a secret that he had been in close contact with Eleanora, his agent's secretary, from the time he went to New York. I was very angry when, two years later, the truth came out that he had been involved with her from the beginning and throughout our dissolution. Even in his last interview a few months before he died, he told a reporter from the *Louisville Courier-Journal* that he had been on his own for two years after moving to New York. I asked him once why he just didn't stay with me, stay sober, and write. "It's too hard," he answered. "It's easier to begin life with someone new."

Dividing the Furniture

We started dissolution proceedings. I wanted to be fair with Walter. Even my mother told me not to try to keep the silver and furniture he had recently inherited from his mother. I sat on the sofa while Walter went through the house on Maplewood Drive choosing paintings and furniture he would have picked up by a van and taken to his apartment in New York. Most of our furniture we had found in antique stores and at auctions and I had refinished them.

From the dining room he chose, from his mother's furniture, a hutch made with inch-thick cherry, and from the living room a cherry drop-leaf table that had belonged to his great-grandmother, a walnut candle table whose top raised to shield the candle from the wind, and a gracious rosewood side chair whose seat I had upholstered.

Once on a shopping trip to Lazarus Department Store in Columbus, Walter had seen an antique chess table that he couldn't resist, one of the few pieces of furniture we had paid a high price for. He promised it to Will. He took that table and two black leather chairs that sat on either side of the fireplace.

I have lived by the belief that people are more important than things, but when I saw those old friends being marked to go to a strange place without me, I didn't take it well. I recalled when we had purchased each piece of furniture, the fun parties we'd had in the living room, and the photograph Walter had taken of Julie and her friend, Adrian, sitting in one of the black chairs when they were in kindergarten.

In fairness, I have to say there was plenty of furniture left, and I soon adjusted to life without the missing pieces. I packed a carton with some of Walter's favorite things: some records, the orange pottery coffee cup made by Will, and some photos. The carton was picked up by the truck that came for the furniture.

I was left the house with the remaining mortgage, most of its furnishings, and the car, which was on its last legs. Walter got all the rights to his literary work and his university retirement funds. We divided our few remaining financial assets. I was grateful to have a secure teaching position with insurance and a retirement plan. Julie was still in college and Walter agreed to help with her expenses.

After the dissolution, my children and I decided not to keep family secrets. Keeping Walter's drinking a secret had prevented me from feeling close to my parents. When we'd visited my parents in Richmond over the years, Walter would stay with his mother, stopping first at the wine store. The children and I stayed with my parents. My parents never asked me about Walter's drinking, but I am sure they questioned the children. My daddy, who was slow to give out compliments, did say one time, "I don't know what is going on, but you have wonderful children."

After Walter left and we adopted the "no-secrets" policy, I was able to feel closer to Mother. I didn't get to feel that way with my dad because he had died in 1970. Will, Julie, and I practice honesty in our relationships. In the years since we implemented the no-secrets policy, Will and Lora got a dissolution of their marriage, and Julie separated from her husband, but we share these kinds of bad times and try to support each other. I was glad for the few years I had with Mother when we could be open and honest. She was from a culture that considered divorce a disgrace as bad as drinking. She didn't tell her friends and relatives that Walter and I were divorced for two years. We became comfortable with each other, and I could ask her questions about her life. I was with her when she died, and there was nothing between us in those last hours that needed to be spoken.

Julie's Wedding/I See Walter for the Last Time

On August 11, 1978, about a year after Walter and I dissolved our marriage, Julie and John McGory were married in Galbreath Chapel on the Ohio University campus. Walter flew in from New York to walk her down the aisle. On the plane he wrote a poem for her and read it at the service. The poem contained references to an airplane trip we had taken during our stay in Mexico when Julie was very small.

We were flying to Puerto Vallarta on a small Mexican plane, and Julie, age three, was in an aisle seat. I noticed her holding out her hand, turning it over and examining it. She looked Will and me over. Then she looked her Dad up and down in the seat across the aisle.

"We are NOT in the air," she said in an angry voice. "My hand is not littler. Daddy is not littler."

She hadn't believed we were flying because we were not getting smaller.

The poem Walter read at the wedding recalled when "Julie was so zippy and so small" on her first plane ride:

I didn't then foresee the thing you'd do.
Turn woman on us all, and be a bride.
And leave me dreaming of the child you were.

The wedding party was at our house on Maplewood Drive. I had spent much of the summer preparing the yard for an outdoor event, but it rained, and we were crowded in the house. My mother came from Richmond, and John's large fam-

Julie, the bride.

ily attended as well as many friends. Walter and I made an extra effort to make the event a pleasant one for Julie.

Walter was calm, but more interested in himself than in the family. He was nervous about being back with his colleagues after his resignation from the university. The house was no longer his house. His mind was in New York. He went through the house and his studio and took books and papers he wanted. An attractive egg cup that had belonged to his grandfather, a quilt a family friend's home economics class had made for Walter when he was born, and a lovely picture of his Aunt Sally as a young girl were items he took from the house that trip.

The morning after the wedding we had breakfast at Frisch's Restaurant. "We will remember my leaving as the best thing I have done," were his parting words. That was the last time I saw Walter. I knew his words to be true, but they were difficult to hear.

Living Alone

Our house on Maplewood had served us for thirteen years until Walter decided to leave for New York. A year later, after Julie got married, I was left alone in a large, empty house.

Will enlarged the studio and put in plumbing, and I rented it to college students to help with household expenses. Over a period of eight years, 35 students shared the house and studio. It was a good experience living with young people from both the United States and other countries. During this time I was busy teaching home economics at Alexander High School and working on a master's degree at Ohio University.

I got the idea that a dog would be a good companion and protection when the students were away on weekends and vacations. I mentioned this at church coffee hour and someone immediately said, "I have just what you need—a half-grown black lab, named Ed Earl, after the sheriff in *The Best Little Whorehouse in Texas*. When I came home after school, Ed Earl wanted to go out to play. I tried taking him to the bedroom with me and tying him to the bedpost until I got a much-needed nap. Once while I was in the bathroom, he went downstairs and deposited in a circle, handful-size poops on the living room floor. Another time I came downstairs to the discouraging sight of the stuffing of my new sofa and the insides of a decapitated stuffed animal covering my living room floor. We definitely were not meant for each other. I gave him back to the owner, and she found him a home where he was much loved by a family with children.

During this time I had little direct contact with Walter. Julie and Will gave me the news they thought I should hear. Walter wrote a children's story for his oldest grandchild, Ryan, called "Turnip Island." It has never been published.

Free To Live Our Own Lives

Through the "Leave it to Beaver" years as a wife and mother, I was always grateful that I had a bachelor's degree and three years of teaching experience to fall back on. I thoroughly enjoyed teaching for a few years, but after a time, I felt stale. I had gone as far as I could go on the salary scale.

I had always wanted a master's degree and had failed in the attempt a couple of times in the home economics department. After a tiring day at school, I had fallen asleep in an afternoon class. I got a C on my first term paper in that department, which one cannot do in graduate school. I picked up the paper, walked out the door, and said to myself, "I never have to go back to that department again." I had lost interest in home economics courses. My degree had served me well for many years, but its time was over.

My mother was in her seventies and still living independently in Kentucky. She told me, "The best years of your life are before you. You have a few years to enjoy life while your health is still good. Make the most of your time."

About this time I heard of a program offered through the philosophy department called "Liberal Studies." Classes were taught on Saturdays. It suited my lifestyle. Before I registered for the course, I went on a university trip to Greece and got credit for writing two papers about the experience. My home economics classes had required projects, not written papers, and I was not sure I could do the required writing. However, I got encouragement from the professor, so I was on my way. In two years I completed the course work. My mother had given me good advice.

When it came time to write a thesis, our professor encouraged us to write about a subject we cared about, so he wouldn't have to nag us to do the work. I had gotten so much encouragement on my papers that I decided to do a creative thesis comparing the lives of three generations of women in my family: my mother's, mine, and my daughter Julie's. Each of us had gone farther because of the life of the other. My mother had made it through the eighth grade. I had a bachelor's degree, and Julie was completing her Ph.D. I was learning to deal with my spelling handicap and was thoroughly enjoying working on my thesis.

I needed to check some facts with Walter, so I sent him a part of my thesis. I hadn't been in contact with him for some time, but finally a letter came in reply to my request. He apologized for keeping my writing so long, but he'd felt guilty towards Eleanora in just having it around. He wrote that he had thought about sending it back unread as getting involved might cause a lot of pain all around.

Anyway, he did read part of it and to my delight said, "I was touched considerably, and amazed at how well you write.

I had no idea. You write with honesty and feeling and a lot of mature self-knowledge." He wrote that he hoped he didn't sound too much like a creative writing teacher. That was exactly what I had wanted him to sound like. Near the end of the letter, Walter commented about a recent visit he'd had from Will and Julie. "I'm so proud of them and love them so much I could burst."

"I think we are both wiser and more grown up for being no longer married. I'm sorry about whatever pain I've caused you, both before and after our marriage ended. You are a good strong woman and deserve the best.

Walter"

The signature with no word of affection to me meant that the emotional part was over.

Julie had been pregnant at the time of that visit to Walter, and at the very end of the letter Walter wrote that he hoped Julie would have a baby girl. On November 8, 1983, Julie gave birth to our second grandson, Ethan James McGory.

CHAPTER 5
WALTER'S DEATH AND MEMORIALS

Lung Cancer

I was having Thanksgiving dinner 1983 with Will, Lora, and Ryan at their house on Sugar Creek. As we were eating, Will casually said, "Dad has cancer. It's in his lungs."

My age group was still healthy, and we didn't hear much about cancer. My thought was that modern medicine and those New York doctors can take care of everything these days. It's probably just a small speck on the x-ray. Walter had been in New York for five years. I was in a singles group and having a few dates, and he seemed very far away.

A friend at coffee hour at church told me that lung cancer spread very rapidly and seldom was treatable by an operation. I realized then that his days were numbered.

The children had been keeping me informed on the progress of his treatment, and I knew he was to be operated on at Sloan-Kettering. The night before the operation, the phone rang. Before picking up the phone, I knew it was Walter. He sounded like his old self and was hopeful that the operation would be a success. The next night he called again, and when I heard his voice I knew that the operation hadn't gone well.

"When I was coming to from the anesthesia, I felt my chest and there were no bandages. I asked the nurse why not and she said there was cancer in my lymph nodes. There was no need to do further surgery."

Through the best and worst of years, there had always been a gut level of truth between us. Sometimes it took a while to get through to it, but when he called, he wanted me to share the depth of his fear.

Will, pregnant Julie, and Walter's sister, Betty, went to see him in the hospital, hoping for some sort of closure. They knew this was the last time they would see him alive. When they got there, they were told not to act as if their father and brother was a dying man. Betty and Julie felt cheated, but Will's last memories of his dad are positive. Will told Walter goodbye and left to catch his plane, but he was too early for the plane, so he returned to the hospital room, and his dad was sleeping peacefully.

There was one note from Walter after that. He wrote that he had finished his fifth of six weeks of radiation and managed to avoid most of the bad side effects so far. "My appetite is good, but I feel as though I could kill for a cigarette. But the craving is getting weaker, thank God, as it did for liquor."

I was at Kenyon College that summer for a six-week workshop. Julie brought baby Ethan to see me. "Dad is dying. He has lost his pretty blond hair, and he will never walk again. Parents are supposed to be there to help their children through our hard times, and now he is leaving us," she cried.

A few days later I was attending a Future Homemakers conference with two of my students. There was a knock on my door early in the morning, and I was told I had a phone call. I knew what the message would be. I left the boys I had brought with me in the care of another teacher and went to spend the day with Julie. There were phone calls back and forth to Eleanora in New York about the funeral arrangements.

We decided Walter's body would be cremated and brought to Richmond for a burial service a week later. It was to be a closed service for Will and Julie and their small children and for a few invited friends. I felt very left out and alone. My friends told me that for the children's sake I should go to the funeral. Pat Elisar, a long time friend from our New Haven days, drove me to Richmond, and we spent the night with my mother.

I got ready early, while Pat and Mother were still asleep. "This is going to be a hard day," I said to myself. I decided to take a walk around Richmond and went by the house where Walter's grandfather, William Thomas, and his children had lived. The present owner was on the porch, and when I told her who I was, she invited me in and showed me around the house. In the front hall was a huge square piano that had belonged to the Tevis family. Around the corner of the street was the cottage where Walter's parents had lived and where we had often visited his widowed mother. I looked in the backyard where Mrs. Tevis had always had a lovely flower garden. Her specialty — iris. The spot was grassed over.

When I returned, Pat, Mother, and Aunt Eliza were ready for the funeral. I had not allowed enough time to get through the traffic on Main Street, so when we arrived for the service they were waiting for us. Michael Kavanaugh gave me his seat. I left Mother in the care of Pat and Aunt Eliza. She was slowly coming along, pointing out her grave site. Six weeks later, October 24, 1984, she was buried there a few yards from Walter's grave.

In early August, when I heard he was dying, I had sent Walter a note: "Your children are populating southeastern Ohio with beautiful grandchildren. Love, Jamie."

Death Notice

This is the note I typed up and copied to mail out to friends to let them know of Walter's death.

August 1984

Yesterday, Walter's ashes were buried in Richmond, Kentucky, in the ancestral plot. Twenty-four close friends and relatives; his children, Will and Julie; his sister, Betty; two of his grandchildren, Ethan and Caleb; and his wife, Eleanora, sat in chairs under a shady fir tree while Father Black, an old friend, read the burial service. I sat in the back row.

Andy, Betty's husband, read a passage from the ending of Walter's novel, *Mockingbird*, of the joyful dying of Spofforth, the most perfect robot ever created. At the line, "He hears the baby squall," a symbol of hope and of the beginning of a new generation of humanity, Will's baby Caleb gave a healthy cry and the mourners responded with a soft laugh at the rightness of it.

John, Julie's husband, read a poem that Walter had written and read at their wedding about Julie being in an airplane in Mexico and disbelieving it, insisting that we were not in the air because we had not grown littler.

Eleanora was sitting on the first seat in
the front row with a wooden box of
ashes about the size of a shoe box beside
her. A ceramic frog was on it. Walter
had a passion for frogs. The undertaker
lowered the box into a two-foot-square
hole. Eleanora crumbled a handful of
dirt over it and broke a yellow rose from
her funeral wreath and dropped it on top
and suggested Will, Julie, and Betty do
the same. They stood and watched the
undertaker fill the hole and cover the
dirt with a square of sod. I stood back
with Lora, Will's wife. It was strange to
see someone else in charge of Walter's
last remains. Eleanora was doing her job
well. The strain of Walter's illness and
death had changed the sparkling person
I had glanced at in the street of New
York in 1978 when we went to the opening of *The Man Who Fell to Earth* to
this intense figure doing the funeral rites
on soil foreign to her.

I broke the etiquette for first wives and
moved up to stand by Will. He moved
close and said, "It will soon be over,
Mom," meaning the burying. "It will
never be over," I said. The cloth of our
lives that we had woven little by little
over the years, the children, the houses
we lived in, friends we knew, jokes we
shared, trips we took, alcohol . . . would
never be over. Painful as it was at times,
it had been our life from the time that he
spoke to me at the teachers' meeting that
first fall day when I was twenty-two and
he twenty-four. There was never a time

when I can say I would have done it differently. In one of the last letters he wrote to me, he said that much of the pain of our marriage was from our differences. I believe these were not just family and background differences. It was also the difference of a man who was alone in the world, *The Man Who Fell to Earth,* and found comfort in a warm earthy type, the Betty Jo's of his books. I took light from his brilliance and he, strength from my soul.

The Lexington Leader called him brilliant and lazy. Father Black called him an ornery lover, and no one would deny that he had been a person full of conflicts. When I saw him five years ago to the day at Julie's wedding, he said that we would look back on his leaving as the best thing he ever did. He got the chance to write full-time, produce five more books, and live his long-dreamed-of life style. I got to grow into a new level of emotional and intellectual maturity, and we both, by the grace of God, were freed from the crippling disease of alcoholism. Those who live near the disease are sucked into the web of ego destruction that it breeds, and I was no exception. As I stood there by Will I felt a sense of release. A restless spirit is put to rest—too soon, it seemed to us who looked on.

There was almost a feeling of summer picnic in the air—Walter's sister, Betty, took flowers off Walter's grave to put on their mother's grave close by. I was glad to see Toby, Michael, Betty, and others that I had not seen for six years. The invited guests from the funeral party went to Boone Tavern in Berea for lunch. While the others went to lunch, Mother, Aunt Liza, Pat Elisar (my friend from years back who knew us when Will and Julie were small), and I took the baby grandsons, Caleb and Ethan, to Mother's apartment. (Ryan, Walter's four-year-old grandson, did not attend.) We were happy to care for them, and it made us feel useful. It took the four of us full time to attend them, and even then we let Ethan get a hard knock on his head from a pan he was playing with, and Aunt Liza gave little Caleb the bottle that was Ethan's.

Mid-afternoon, Will and Lora and Julie and John came to pick up the babies, packed up, and headed home. While Pat and Mother ate a snack, I drove back to the cemetery and put a yellow rose from Walter's garden on his grave.

Thinking of Walter in past times is something that I will have to get used to.

Jamie

Jamie Tevis

Remembering Walter Tevis

The night before Walter's memorial service at Galbreath Chapel on the Ohio University campus, Dan Nather interviewed several of Walter's colleagues for an obituary in *The Athens News*. For the most part, I feel it gives an honest reflection of how he was viewed among his peers.

"Remembering Walter Tevis" From *The Athens News*, September 27, 1984, by Dan Nather, *The Athens News* Arts writer:

Former Ohio University English professor Walter Tevis can probably best be described as a man of conflicts. He had resolved what was his greatest conflict before he died of lung cancer on August 9 in New York; he was becoming the writer he wanted to be.

While he was teaching on campus from 1965 to 1978, he was tremendously well liked and admired as both a teacher and a companion. "He had an extraordinarily austere view of what could be done with stories," said OU English professor Jack Matthews in a memorial service for Tevis yesterday.

OU English professor Reid Huntley offered a demonstration of this in recalling a critique Tevis wrote for a story Huntley had written. Tevis' instructions were simple: "Xerox your manuscript. You don't want to deface your original. Take the Xerox, and cut mercilessly."

He also gave some sound advice to

Huntley's pedagogy class in 1972. Some of it included:

"Throw away the first four pages."

"Learn to fight past page seven."

"What you are trying to sweep under the rug may be where the story is."

"Read. Read. Read. Your virgin mind won't be damaged by it. Literature is not, in itself, a spontaneous, self-generating act."

Matthews remembers him as "very critical about his own defects. He would tell you what he thought. He would clear the air when obfuscation was present." He also had "very lofty ideals concerning literature," Matthews said.

Ohio University history professor Don Richter, Tevis' chess partner for four years, says of Walter: "His real passion was chess, not pool."

"He was not a cautious player," Richter said. "He was an attacking player, as I was. We got into some bizarre situations."

Richter spoke of a tour they took together in London. "We would go outside the home of one of the poets," Richter said, "and he would just start reciting poetry off the top of his head. It was wonderful to be with him."

Daniel Keyes still remembers his first contact with Tevis after coming to OU in 1966. "When I came into town, (Tevis) phoned me and said, 'Welcome to Athens. I'm your new colleague. Let's go out and have a beer.' He was a very generous man."

But there was pain in this seemingly happy existence. Tevis lived to write, and he did very little writing during his tenure at OU. As a result, he took up these various intellectual pursuits and drank heavily, a habit that began on his sojourn in Mexico. He was also a heavy smoker.

"He just wanted to be doing things," Jamie, his former wife, said. "When everybody had gone home and there wasn't anything left for him to do, he read for a while and then went to bed, often after 2 in the morning.

"He had no preservation or consistency about his life, so there was no energy left for writing."

Tevis' friend Victor Goedicke also saw the problems he was having. "(Tevis) got more mileage per hour than any writer I've ever known," Goedicke said. "The problem was getting started. It was a psychological holdback."

Several faculty members visited him in New York in the spring of 1983. "He was the happiest I had ever seen him," Huntley said.

"He (had) just needed a change to get back to work," Keyes said. "He hurt a lot of people, but when he moved up to New York, he came back to life."

Jamie was especially hurt by his move

which also meant moving far from his grown children, Will and daughter Julie Tevis McGory.

I don't like the way he did it," Jamie said, "in that he left me out of it. But I'm very glad he did it."

Tevis had told Keyes earlier this year that he was "very, very eager" to write a sequel to *The Hustler*. It was recently published under the title *The Color of Money*. It would be his last published work.

His heavy smoking had taken its toll. He was discovered to have lung cancer early this year, and began radiation treatments. The cancer was reduced, but it soon spread to his lymph nodes. He was hospitalized on June 16, and never left the hospital. He married Eleanora Walker a few weeks before his death on Aug. 9.

Goedicke knew that Tevis had a lot of tragedy in his life. "He spent all his life trying to settle into an environment that suited him. I think the New York life came closer than anything else he tried."

Had he lived, Goedicke said, Tevis would have spent this weekend in a cabin at Royal Oaks with his son Will, just "to rusticate and enjoy nature and visit Will."

At yesterday's memorial service, Keyes read Tevis' short story "Far From Home," and closed with these remarks: "He left behind his traces far from

home, but as long as I have his novels
and stories to read, I won't have to say
good-bye to him."

Jamie's Comments on Mr. Nather's Article in *The Athens News*

Mr. Nather, on the night before the memorial service at the Galbreath Chapel, interviewed several of Walter's colleagues. I felt it was an informative view of what his life here at Ohio University had been like. Walter was well liked and an interesting person to know. The faculty lounge was his favorite place—where he could get a cup of coffee and always a listening ear. I would like to add a few comments on the article.

He tells Professor Huntley's class to "Throw away the first four pages." Good advice to a group of wannabe writers. In truth, Walter threw away hardly any of his writing—at least in the beginning when he was turning out short stories and *The Hustler*. He would get an idea and let it develop in his head like a puzzle. He didn't talk about his story as he was writing it, believing it took from his ability to put it on paper. He wrote very few things that didn't get published. His manuscripts have a few corrections, but not much went into the trash can. When his writing was going well it flowed, like Fats or Fast Eddie when they got a long run at the pool table.

He began writing in the days of the typewriter and carbon paper. He was a master hunt-and-peck—not a touch typist. Even his last books were written before the days of computers.

Walter believed a writer needed talent, and hard work

alone was not enough to produce publishable works. In his latter days, he did admit that he couldn't tell the difference in what he wrote when inspired and when he just wrote to get the job done. He admitted that good writing takes talent, skills, practice, as well as character. Does this sound like the qualities needed for a winning game of chess and pool?

Professor Huntley and Professor Keyes make it appear in the *News* article that what Walter had to do to find happiness was to change scenes (and wives) and take up the pen and write. These changes did help, but he finally faced the demons and scars of his life that alcohol had covered for the major part of his life. As he drank more, he talked more and wrote less.

Walter fell back on teaching at one point in his career and for many years thoroughly enjoyed the academic life. Teaching came easy for him, but in the back of his mind he knew he should be writing. He was a "talking writer," making appearances because of his fame from *The Hustler*, but not producing new work.

All during that time he was saying, "I'm not doing what I'm meant to do. I should be writing, and maybe there is nothing in me left to say."

Letters of Condolence

This note is from Walter's boyhood friend, Toby Kavanaugh.

Aug. 27, 1984
Lexington

Dear Jamie,

I was so pleased to receive your journal and note. Your prose and description were excellent—informative and poignant. Some of Walter's talent has surely rubbed off on you.

I hope you can decipher my print—no typewriter for some unknown reason—and even the bank can't decipher my longhand.

When one lives in the same home for 55 years and has had the same job for 35 years, he knows those are signs of a very conservative person. Not being fond of change, death (the biggest change) is harder for me to accept. Also, a single person depends more on his few close friends.

Although distance and circumstances had prevented Walter and me from having much contact in the last few years, <u>he was always my best friend</u>.

I guess this would have been even harder on both of us if we had been in close contact with Walter every day in the last few years.

My memories of you two in Carlisle, Irvine, etc. All seem good to me though I realize there were problems—mostly alcohol, I guess.

Sorry I didn't get to see and talk to you more when you were here. Please call or write soon. Fill me in on the last years and what you and family are doing now.

I was very proud of Will and Julie. You did a great job of raising them—and Walter too!

Love,
Toby

Ten years after Toby wrote me this letter, he was found dead in his driveway. It was thought a robber had come to rob him and not expected Toby to return at 2 in the morning. He had been hit on the head. More than five years after Toby's murder, there was a flurry of police activity on the case. Briefly there was a suspect, but soon an unassailable alibi was discovered, and the case has never been solved. During those recent events, the newspaper articles identified Toby as the man who taught Walter Tevis to play pool. That was forty years after

The Hustler appeared.

The following letter of condolence was from an old friend of Walter's, Frank Mathias. They had met in college classes at the University of Kentucky. Their friendship continued when we lived in Carlisle — Frank's home town. One afternoon Frank and I shared a seat on the bus from Lexington. Frank was a history buff, and the conversation led to World War II. He asked me if I remembered where I was when Pearl Harbor was attacked. We shared memories all the way home. A little later, Frank told Walter, "You should consider asking that young lady to marry you."

Frank brought Florence, his future wife, to visit us in Lexington. We have kept in touch through the years. He recently wrote a book, *The G.I. Generation,* published by University of Kentucky Press, about growing up in the quiet little (Mayberry) town of Carlisle and sent me a copy.

Friday, Aug. 16, 1984

Dear Jamie,

Florence and I were shocked and saddened very much by Walter's rather unexpected death (we knew nothing of his lung condition), and even more by his life style of the past few years.

Your description of Walter's funeral and of past places and people in your lives was wonderful, and we thank you very much for remembering us with a copy. My memories of Carlisle thirty-two years ago are vivid: Walter's living with Tom Abraham, Caroll Hall and the trailer on Dorsey Avenue, the old high school building which is now being torn down, etc. Then your marriage and the house or apt. on North street and Walter selling his first story to *Esquire.* He was so excited—weren't we all! I first met Walter in Tom Stroup's John Milton class at UK in the summer of 1949. Walter was such a pest with questions to which he knew the answer that Stroup gave him a "D." We sat together and soon were drinking beer together at Rose Street and other spots. He liked the idea that I played in Bob Bleidt's dance band. Later in Carlisle I tried to teach him to play clarinet but it was hopeless. I think I showed up in *The Hustler* as the clarinet player in Louisville. Then it was off to Irvine, by which time I was peddling promotional material and samples for Lorillard tobacco company. I remember staying with you there—smuggling in beer and cigarette samples to a dry county. (I quit smoking in 1967.) I returned to UK to work on a doctorate and found the Tevises there, with Walter working as an engineering editor I think. Then he sat down and wrote *The Hustler*—wasn't that in the basement of your house over on Harrodsburg Road? In any event, Mexico followed, alcohol, and all the rest. Walter was a unique individual in intellectual brilliance, but still heir to the same old failings of the flesh like all the rest of us. The combination in one person, I think, made him the fine writer he was and also the extremely interesting person and conversationalist he certainly was. It also, I suppose from your letter, made him very hard to live with at times.

Jamie, come see us. The kids all live on campus, and we have a four-bedroom house. Come and spend a day or two.

May God's blessings be with you and the children <u>always</u>.

Sympathy and Love from Frank and Florence Mathias

Conversations with Walter

Reid Sinclair, a bachelor from Virginia, came to the Ohio University English department in 1965, the same year as Walter. The three of us joined the church discussion group where Reid met Stephanie, a single mother of two small children. They married, and in a few short years Reid, the bachelor, was the father of four children of his own and two step-children. Reid and I became members of the Episcopal church and planned faculty picnics. We felt a kinship because of our southern backgrounds. The Tevises, the Sinclairs, and the Fitches from our New Haven days became good friends. Walter and I became godparents for one of the Sinclair children. Reid often came by our house with one of the children in tow to watch football games with Walter. Reid now lives in Athens. All our children are grown, but we still rely on each other's friendship. I asked him to write his memories of Walter.

Conversations with Walter, by Reid Sinclair

One Sunday afternoon prior to my marriage, Walter and I were talking—and probably watching football—at my small garage apartment—the temperature was far below zero. Suddenly there were cracks and hisses in the garage below—the pipes had broken; water was shooting through the garage. Good talk interrupted.

We had, to borrow a phrase, good talk. After the eighty-mile drive back to Athens on the birth of my first child, I stopped by the Tevises'. Walter was reading the encyclopedia. We talked until the early hours of Monday morning.

One evening after work I invited Walter by for an end-of-the-day drink. My wife kept doing this and that and didn't join us, as was her custom. After a bit, she came in and said calmly, "Reid, my folks are on the way over to pick up the children—you will need to take me to the hospital." End of that good talk.

I left Athens—for nine years—before Walter left, as a resident—forever. We loved literature, and we were, in our quite different fashions, writers, but we exchanged, I believe, only two or three letters over those years from 1970 until his death in 1984.

187

A Look Back at Irvine's "Ichabod" by William Neikirk

William Neikirk, one of Walter's high school students when we were teaching at Irvine, became a writer for the *Chicago Tribune* and wrote this article after Walter's death. It was carried in several papers, and of all the articles written about his death, I think this says it the best.

WASHINGTON—When I was a high school sophomore in Irvine, Ky., in the late 1950's, my classmates couldn't restrain their laughter the first time they saw our new English teacher.

He was in his 20s, but he was certainly no Robert Redford. He was tall, thin and ungainly, and he obviously had not seen an orthodontist. His appearance evoked the worst instincts in a rather cruel band of boisterous and immature teenagers.

Soon he acquired the behind-the-back nickname of Ichabod Crane after the fictional Washington Irving character who eventually met up with the Headless Horseman.

Our Ichabod had a hard time controlling a rambunctious class. But, oh, would he teach! And tell stories. He told about playing poker and pool and how he had worked in a pool hall to help pay his way through the University of Kentucky. He loved sports, which seemed funny and anomalous to us, considering his unathletic look. He introduced us to Shakespeare and made us understand why the Bard was so great.

More than anything else, he loved to talk about writing. On occasion, he would mention that he had been published in a few magazines, but few took him seriously or regarded this news very highly. What would an accomplished writer be doing teaching in a small town in Nowheresville? He shared with us the difficulty of writing, the loneliness of it, the sweat, blood and tears of it, as well as the requirements of getting published.

He was good with basics, but he viewed the mechanics of writing only as a means to an end. He tried to teach us a little of the feel of it, but it mostly went over our heads. Still, he had that ring of authority about writing. My first writing attempt for him came back marked brightly in red, and I strove hard in later papers to try to please him.

Because he talked about pool and gambling, he was not exactly popular with some uptight folks in our small town, but as far as I know there was never any pressure to remove him. Indeed, our Ichabod left on his own for another job somewhere in the Kentucky Highway Department, I believe. Most of us were sad to see him go, not only because of the storytelling but because a main target of our teenage cruelty was no longer in our midst. We thought we would never hear from him again.

As a student at the University of Kentucky, I passed by the poolroom where he had told us he'd worked, and I remembered those high school English classes fondly. Soon after that, I learned he had written a book.

It was about pool, gambling, and Minnesota Fats. It was called *The Hustler*, and was made into a movie with Paul Newman, Jackie Gleason, and Piper Laurie. It was fantastic. When I saw some of my old high school classmates later and talked about our former teacher's success, they looked at our Ichabod quite differently. What they had seen as amusing they now found wonderful and admirable. Some who had not heard a word he had said all that sophomore year now professed that he was the best teacher they had ever had.

Although our Ichabod wondered about making a living through writing, he had "manufactured" a product that made a lot of money for a lot of people, including himself. He did it through talent and the effective appropriation of his experiences.

So much of our economic thinking focuses on the mechanical selling of goods and services, not the vastly more important creative thinking that goes behind it. In our new communications economy, those who are able to think and innovate are more important than ever. And that means education is crucial.

After *The Hustler*, our man went on to write *The Man Who Fell to Earth*, which also was made into a movie, and became a professor at Ohio University. He gave up teaching in 1978 and devoted all his time to writing fiction.

Walter Tevis was his name, but he was by now our Ichabod, the man who had blessed our sophomore class one year with his presence and was no longer a target of youthful ridicule. It was with sadness that we all learned that he died Aug. 9, of lung cancer, in New York.

*I got a wonderful feeling of lightness at leaving
behind the clutter of our lives.*
Jamie.

CHAPTER 6
RECOVERY

I Move to a New House

After Walter left for New York I continued to teach home economics at Alexander High School. I lived in our house on Maplewood for six years after our separation. After I got my master's degree, I decided to put the house up for sale. It sold within a week. I called Will and said, "What am I going to do? I didn't expect it to sell so fast."

Will said, "Let it go. You can find some place to live. It may be a long time before you get another offer." There were not many houses for sale in my price range and size. I found one that would suit me and made a bid. The owner said, " I don't think we are ready to sell. We were thinking of getting a divorce, but now we don't know if we will or not." There was a small house on Ohio Avenue that needed a lot of refurbishing. The street was known as Widow's Lane because at one time thirty-five widows lived on it. It was never my intention to join them, but I thought, "In a pinch it will do and I am almost a widow since my ex-husband died. I will paint the walls white, and it will hold my furniture until I find something more suitable." Because it was the last house of an estate waiting to be settled, I got it on a low first bid. I hired a crew of workmen who roofed, sided, plumbed, wired, and made it like new.

I had a giant yard sale — going through the garage, attic and basement, telling each item, "If you are going with me you have to be useful or good to look at." I got a wonderful feeling of lightness at leaving behind the clutter of our lives. I moved in 1986, planted trees, made a garden, added a deck and made room in the basement for one renter, whose rent check pays most of the utilities. When Julie comes with her family, I rent them a room in a nearby motel with a swimming pool. For larger family gatherings we go to Will's or Julie's house.

Thoughts on Celebrity

One might think that having a book accepted for a movie would mean "Hollywood, here I come." This is not what happens. From the time the contract is signed for the book rights, the film director and producer make the decisions. The author has no say in the way the movie is made. We were in Mexico when *The Hustler* was being filmed, and we read in the paper who the actors were going to be. Fortunately, first-rate, box office name actors were chosen: Paul Newman, Jackie Gleason, George C. Scott, and Piper Laurie. Walter did see some of the filming, and I remember him saying that Piper Laurie kept muffing her lines and the scene had to be shot over and over. Movie making is hard work, and there is no time to be impressed with the author of the book standing around on the set.

When we saw the movie for the first time in New York, and the dialogue Walter had written was coming out of the actors' mouths on the big screen, it was an eerie feeling. Charlie was saying words I might have said. The story followed the book until Piper Laurie's character kills herself near the end.

Walter did go to New Mexico to be on the set of *The Man Who Fell to Earth*. I think he stood around and drank a lot of beer and hung out with the director's wife and with David Bowie when he wasn't on the set. Walter brought home a foot of 2x4 board from the set autographed for Julie by David Bowie. Later in the filming process, David wrote Walter a letter. The stationery he used was interesting because there was a photo-copied thumb on it, as though someone was handing the letter to you. The letter reported that the filming was going well. The letter was signed "Kindest regards, David."

Walter said that David Bowie was a very kind, gentle man.

Walter enjoyed the excitement of being on the set where the movie was in the making, especially after the book had been out of circulation for almost fifteen years. Artie Shaw had bought the movie rights and held them for years but nothing came of his intentions. In 1975 Lion International bought the movie rights and Nicolas Roeg directed the filming of it.

The closest I ever came to a movie star was when Paul Newman came to Ohio University for a political rally. He came to campaign for Eugene McCarthy, and of course we went to hear him speak. I was surprised that he was not as tall as he appears in films, but he has the most wonderful blue eyes—as blue as the ocean.

As I was preparing this book, I wrote to Paul Newman on a long shot, knowing that he is a very busy man. Several weeks later I was thrilled to find a long manila envelope in my mailbox, "PAUL NEWMAN" on the back and no return address. I had asked if he would comment on playing Eddie in *The Hustler*. His answer was, "Yes. What do you want me to say?" I was delighted. I sent him some questions about things related to *The Hustler*, and he sent me thoughtful replies. It had been forty-two years since *The Hustler* came to the screen, and Mr. Newman had played many roles since that time. I appreciated his attention to the matter that had been such a small part of his long and famous career, but which had been such an important part of our lives. Here are four of the questions I asked, followed by Mr. Newman's answers:

Q: Why did you agree to play the role of
Eddie in The Hustler?

A: The background for "The Hustler"
had never been seen on the screen before and all of the characters were richly
defined and especially, "Eddie," who
had several spiky trajectories. Always an
interesting challenge for an actor.

Q: Were the pool shots yours?

A: I took the dining room table out of
our apartment and put in a pool table
and Willie Mosconi was my teacher. A
few shots weren't mine, but certainly
not very many.

Q: What was it like working with Jackie
Gleason?

A: Gleason kept his distance offstage,
but on the set, he was a real pro.

Q: How was your life affected by making the two movies—The Hustler and
The Color of Money?

A: I don't know of any specific impact
on my life as a result of The Color of
Money or The Hustler except whenever
I'm in a place where there's a pool table,
I almost always get hustled. And it's
their entreaty: "Hey, we don't have to
play for much—what do you want to
play for?" I look them straight in the eye

and say, "How about your house?"—
that has always collapsed the challenge
and kept my bank account intact.

The movie version of *The Man Who Fell to Earth* pretty well followed the book, but *The Color of Money* mostly used only Walter's name and characters, although he was paid a good sum for the book. Someone else wrote the screen play. I recall reading that Walter was paid $250,000 for the movie rights. Walter died before the movie came to the screen.

The following story is hearsay on my part since this was after my time in Walter's life. Walter had the idea for a sequel to *The Hustler* after he moved to New York. He contacted Paul Newman and persuaded him to make another movie. Walter reported that he, Paul, and Joanne Woodward met for lunch in New York. Joanne wanted to talk about horses as Walter was from Kentucky. I was curious to know more about that meeting so I included a question about it in my letter to Paul Newman. His response: "I don't remember meeting with Walter for lunch," and then he graciously added, "but I have a memory like a sieve." I have no reason not to believe Walter's version of the New York lunch. My interpretation is that it was much more exciting for Walter to meet with Paul Newman, than it was for Paul Newman to meet Walter.

Ohio University brings in famous people for speeches and public appearances. The one I enjoyed most was Pearl Buck, who came to Athens to premiere a movie about her life. The faculty in the creative writing department and their spouses were invited to President Alden's home to have dinner with her. After dinner she sat by the fireplace in a long yellow gown with her white hair done in a bun on the top of her head. At her crossed, tiny feet sat her young paramour who had produced the movie of her life. It was showing first in Athens because we are close to West Virginia, the place of her birth.

We all went over to the movie theater to see the movie which was not very entertaining. I later read where she said what a joy it was to find love later in life.

On another occasion we were invited to the president's home to have dinner with Alex Haley, the author of *Roots*. We went over to the auditorium to hear him tell about how his search had led him to Africa. He gave a spellbinding speech, hardly pausing for breath. He kept us on the edge of our seats. I later heard him at another event, and he gave the exact same speech which I enjoyed as much as the first time I heard it even though I could anticipate the punch lines.

Many famous people come to Athens. Once on the way to the grocery store, I saw President Nixon getting off the plane at the University airport, and I heard President Johnson speak on the College Green. President Jimmy Carter spoke to a packed auditorium, and I couldn't get a seat, but I listened on closed-circuit television from the student center.

There is something that makes us want to touch the hem of celebrities' garments. For years I was the wife of Walter Tevis, who wrote books that were made into movies, and then I was the mother of Will and Julie. I decided that I wanted to be noted for my own worth. One night I was reading a play script for a small part in one of the summer theater productions. I remember the exact moment when I decided I was going to devote my time to the arts. I had spent my life up to this point following my Baptist upbringing to go forth and do good. Such thinking had led me to marry someone who needed me at the time. I tried to save him from alcoholism and failed. When I saw my name posted for the mayor's wife role in "Bye Bye, Birdie," I was delighted. All I had to do was sit backstage for most of the play, come on stage, and faint in the mayor's arms when Birdie came on stage.

For a few summers, I got minor parts in the summer theater, went to Greece to see the antiquities, earned a master's degree, and began writing. Another fun thing I do is interview interesting people and show the programs on the public television station. This is a team project I do with my friend Joe Agranoff. We did these interviews once a week for ten years, and now we mostly depend on reruns to have something to put on the air. We need a new digital camera, but I think it is not the cost that is stopping us — it's the fact that we have to learn to use the new buttons and to adapt it to the computer.

I sing with two groups, "Home Remedy" and "The Late Bloomers." The Late Bloomers are just two old women who took up singing on the porch of a restored log village on the campus of a vocational college. People liked what we do and started asking us to appear at local functions. Helen, my partner in Late Bloomers, plays harmonica and dulcimer. I play guitar and we both sing. Our latest performances were at an assisted living home and at a newly restored opera house. Sometimes we get paid and sometimes we sing for free. It is fun either way. There are six of us in the "Home Remedy" band. We perform for fairs, churches, and festivals. We have also produced two CD's.

I am busy enough that about once a week someone says, "I keep up with you through the paper." I taught over a thousand students during my teaching years. One of them speaks to me most every time I go out.

Most of the people I see are too young to remember *The Hustler*. I am my own person. I like it that way.

Old Friends and Transitions

Last week (2002), I attended an Elderhostel in Boston, and while there I met with my old friends, Joe and Jackie Vilimas. Although we have kept in touch, we had not seen each other for many years. They visited us at a writers' conference in the

60's on Cape Cod where Walter was one of the instructors. After the children were grown, we spent a week with them in Maine in 1973. We were all in good health then.

Our bodies now showed the passing of time. Joe was walking with a limp, had heart problems, and was wearing a hearing aid. Jackie had had a stroke, had fallen and broken her pelvis in three places, and walked with a cane. My scars were less visible—a heart valve, two operations, arthritis, and aching feet and joints. As it is with old friends, however, it seemed no time had passed at all.

We met at Pier Four, a seafood restaurant, and afterwards Joe drove us to their home to spend the afternoon. We sat in their attractive living room that Jackie had decorated with bright paintings, art objects, and crystal vases. Oriental rugs highlighted the shiny parquet floors. The effect was more attractive than any of the museums I had visited during my week with the Elderhostel. We relaxed, recalling events from our days in Mexico and the holidays we had shared when they lived in Boston and we in New Haven. The children, Will, Julie, and Joanna, were in elementary school, riding their bikes, playing with Barbie dolls, and throwing rocks at the ocean. Those were the Kennedy Camelot days when all the country was full of hope. They came to be with us for Thanksgiving a few days after John Kennedy was killed.

While we relaxed, we shared news of our children. Will and Julie have given me six grandchildren. The bouncy Joanna I first knew in Mexico found rearing three children too much for her, and Joe and Jackie have taken her teenagers into their home. I was glad to get to meet them and found it endearing that Joanna had named two of them Joe and Jackie, after her parents. Catherine she named for her grandmother.

They treated me to dinner at a revolving restaurant overlooking the Charles River where Harvard youths were sculling, making a lovely picture. As the restaurant turned, we could see all of Boston. The John Hancock building I had gone to the top of with the Elderhostel group was in view. After dinner, Joe put me in a cab to return to my group at the hotel. (Driving in Boston is almost impossible because of the Big Dig.) We promised to keep in touch more often.

A few days after I returned to Athens, Will called to say he was coming by to find an old home movie of his dad. A company in California was putting *The Hustler* on DVD and wanted pictures for a documentary to follow the film. He mowed the yard while I prepared lunch for us — a salad with beets and turnip, two of Will's favorite foods. The hour with Will was like old times when he still lived at home. We have always enjoyed the company of each other, but our lifestyles seldom give us the opportunity to be together for long, although he lives only twenty minutes away.

We talked about the recent wedding of his son Ryan to Melissa Phurmond. Julie, looking like she was straight from New York with her fashionable short haircut and leopard print blouse, was there with Jonathan, fifteen, and Elizabeth, twelve. Will and his wife Natalie, with the help of friends, had put up a huge white tent with white covered tables decorated with flowers in Will's handmade pots. On the outside wall of the shop where the food was being served, Will had hung framed pictures from Ryan's early days and pictures of the family, including his dad and me with Will and Julie when we were in Mexico. More than two hundred guests divided into four lines around the two heavily laden tables after stopping to view the pictures. Couples danced on the basketball court to songs from the Beatles' era until midnight.

As Will was leaving he said, "My children are leaving, and I am having trouble adjusting. Ryan is married, and Caleb, seventeen, lives with his mother. Adrienne will be sixteen in October. When we have children, we are hardly more than children ourselves, and by the time we learn how to be parents, they are gone."

"It is a hard period of time when our children leave

home," I answered. "You married, Julie went to college, and Walter went to New York at about the same time. It is hard, but you can do it. After a time the children return with children, and the cycle begins all over. It is a time of new beginnings."

I read recently where someone said these passages in our lives, such as divorce and when the children leave home, are like when all the elastic in our underwear gives way at once. Divorce is difficult for all of us. Even Madeline Albright of the U.S. State Department said in an Oprah interview, "I was wiped out for a year and then I had to take charge of my life and move on."

I think Julie found leaving John and her home was harder than she had imagined. The last time I talked to her she said the children would be gone for ten days with their dad to attend their uncle's wedding and for a trip through the Smokies.

"I will not see them for ten whole days," she said.

Now that I am older and look back on my life, I am grateful for those single years. Like the old song says, "You must walk that lonesome valley. You must walk it by yourself. No one else can walk it for you. You must walk it by yourself."

Jamie's Letter to Walter (March 2002)

Walter,

We tend to think that a relationship is closed when a marriage ends or when a loved one dies. Some people go to their spouse's graves and talk to them. (They go in secret so people won't think them crazy.) The emotional part of our relationship ended long ago. After going through the scrapbook—pictures, clippings, and letters—I see that our lives make a story: not a perfect one, but it was our story. The story will continue through the lives of our children's children.

Death is so final. It would be pleasant to sit over coffee at Woolworth's or Frisch's and catch you up on our lives here in Athens, Ohio. The restaurants are no longer here either. When we parted in front of Frisch's Restaurant twenty-four years ago when you were here for Julie's wedding, you said we would find your leaving was the best thing you ever did. Your going was long overdue but nevertheless painful and deceitful. Giving up a marriage is something like giving up on a 9x12 needlepoint rug. One is aware it has flaws but finds it hard to quit after all the work that went into it. I can now say you were right. Our life together had run its course.

I am now seventy-two years old, retired after teaching for seventeen years at Alexander High School. After you left I got a master's degree from Ohio University, and would you believe it, became a writer, self-publishing two books, selling lots of magazine articles and writing a column for the Richmond newspaper.

You have six very special grandchildren, but Ryan is the only one you saw. He is twenty-three and married to Melissa — still very handsome — takes after his mother's family in looks, and still has his one dimple.

Ellis Hall, where you used to teach, has been remodeled, and Will got the contract for the heating and cooling. Ryan did much of the work. He said, "I bet I got more money for my work than my grandfather got for teaching there." I told Ryan he was right.

Four years after Ryan came Caleb, and fifteen months later Adrienne. Remember how Will enjoyed the Andy Griffith shows? Will and Opie were born on the same day and are the same age, forty-nine, this year. He took his parenting skills from Andy and is a wonderful parent. Caleb, Will's second son, is an excellent golfer. He was invited to compete in a golf tournament in Europe in 2002, and came in third out of 100 players. Adrienne plays on the first volleyball team and is an

Melissa and Ryan (above).

Will and Natalie (above).

Let's see who is taller!
Will and Julie (right).

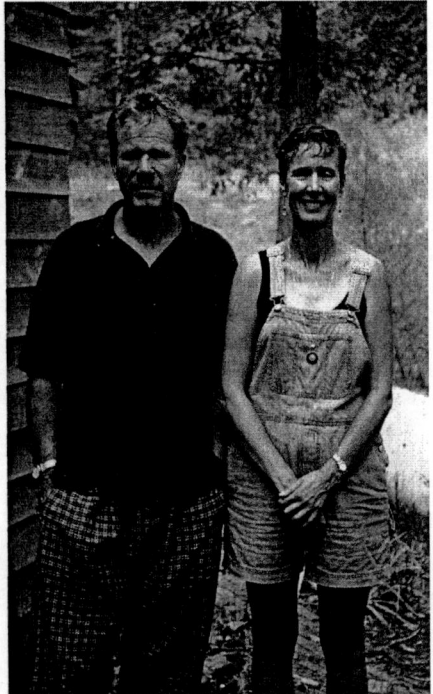

excellent pitcher for her baseball team at Athens High. Both are regulars on the honor roll.

Julie has a Ph.D. from Ohio State and does research in languages and travels to give workshops, the most recent in New Zealand. She has three children: Ethan, nineteen; Jonathan, seventeen; and Elizabeth, fourteen. Jonathan takes after you the most, has curly hair and is tall and thin — 6'4. I took a picture of Caleb and Jonathan in your old Navy uniform. Both boys have to bend down to give me a hug.

After twenty-two years of marriage, Julie and John are separating. Julie is struggling with a mid-life crisis. I helped her buy a house near the house she is leaving so they can both be near the children. Ethan plays stand-up bass in the Columbus Youth Orchestra. Ethan and his friends have a band. They entered their CD in a contest and were selected as one of the ten best out of two hundred contestants. They are invited to play at Lincoln Center in New York. Ethan will be attending Dennison this fall. Jonathan plays drums for the high school marching band and is active in the drama department at his high school. Elizabeth is in middle school, plays volleyball, likes animals and wants to be a veterinarian. They are a fine bunch of kids. You would enjoy knowing them. I have tried to get at least one of them to do a class paper on you with no luck so far.

To the grandchildren you are a legend. When Will is carving a chicken or turkey, he will sometimes jokingly say as you so often said, "My father never taught me how to carve a chicken," remembering how you butchered the bird — refusing to look into a book and learn.

Of course, we can't see an artichoke without saying, "Did you know an artichoke is kin to a thistle?" I went to Greece and thistles are growing all over the country.

You used to quote your Aunt Sallie, "Papa loved sad cake." I found a recipe and made it for Sunday dinner at Will's and told the children about Papa. They know he was your great-grandfather, was one of Morgan's Raiders, and was the owner of a gold-headed cane given him by a Kentucky governor. He is the one with the tall monument in the Richmond cemetery with the names of his three wives on the sides. Natalie noted that Lucy and her baby died on the same day. One of his wives was the owner of the "Bell Root" silver serving spoon that your mother gave me for my first Christmas in the family. Will and Natalie now have it as well as the Tevis dishes that came with the family from Oklahoma.

I asked my niece Gwen's daughter, Anne, if she remembered you. She said, "The cat pooped in his red sheepskin slippers. He put his foot into it and then threw the shoe out the window." So much for fame.

The large, old, rambling house on Maplewood that you bought sight unseen got very empty with you and the children gone. I bought and fixed up a little house on Ohio Ave. and have a dog. I have been here for sixteen years. I painted the door frame purple and two yard chairs to match. It's almost like having a swing on the front porch. I sit in the front yard and play Scrabble with my friend Joe Agranoff and watch the neighbors jogging, skating, bicycling, dog walking, and taking late-afternoon strolls. I used to call the street Widows' Lane, but now that I am single it suits me perfectly.

I am single, but Joe is a very special friend. Joe came from Cincinnati to be near his grandchildren several years ago, and I met him at a Christmas party at the Richters. We hit it off from the beginning and enjoy similar things: auctions, books, "Barney Miller" and "Andy Griffith" reruns, and food. I cook meals for us at home, and he takes us out often. He is good company and we enjoy the same movies. Last summer we went for a cruise on the Mississippi on the *Delta Queen*. We get along quite well despite the fact that he is Jewish, reared in Brooklyn, and I am an Episcopalian raised as a Southern Baptist.

I asked Will what he would want to tell you if he could. He was very thoughtful and then said, "I think of Dad a lot, especially when I am working with tools. (He has a sizable heating and cooling business.) When Dad and I were working on a project we had to do several steps to put in screws, bore a hole with a bit, then change the bit and make another place for the screw head. Now they have drills that do all that for you and, in reverse, they can remove old screws. They have magnetic hammers that hold the nails, leaving your hand free." Then we both laughed at how you were always forgetting where you laid your tools and how your jeans fell off from the weight of things in your pockets. Will would tell you he has become a reader as you wished him to be.

Will is very happy — not driven by conflicts as was your life. He has a lot of influence in the Jehovah Witness Fellowship. After he and Lora divorced, Will married a pretty young woman, Natalie Tromm. She wears my wedding ring. Sometimes I see it on her hand and remember how I went into the street in front of the house and cried out loud when I took it off the day of the dissolution. I recall we went uptown in Carlisle at recess and bought our rings at the jewelry store. You didn't have the money and I paid for them — $7 and $9.

In your science fiction you talked of cameras that developed pictures on the spot. Now there are digital cameras that project the pictures directly on the computer screen. Remember Betty Craddock from our church group? She can see her grandchild's pictures from China minutes after they are taken. This cyberspace-age has taken us farther than even you ever imagined. Scientists have cloned a sheep named Dolly, and they say they are able to clone human beings.

After all these years, your books are still in the stores and movie reviews are on the internet. Just last week *The Man Who Fell to Earth* was reviewed in the Ohio University *Post*, and *The Hustler* was on TV. Scholars will be doing research on you for years to come. The reviews say you were a brilliant writer and a very creative thinker.

It is said a person is never truly dead as long as someone

Life can be fun after 60!
Joe Agranoff and Jamie.

Aren't we a jolly bunch?!
(from top) Elizabeth McGory, Adrienne Tevis, Jonathan McGory, Ryan Tevis, Ethan McGory, and Caleb Tevis

"Our children are populating Southeast Ohio."

(from back left) Julie Tevis McGory, Ryan Tevis, Jonathan McGory, Ethan McGory, Caleb Tevis, Will Tevis, Natalie Tevis and Adrienne Tevis

(from front left) Anne Pittman and Gwen Pittman Lehman (nieces), Jamie Griggs Tevis, Elizabeth McGory, Chi Pittman Inegia

remembers. You will remember the tablecloth we painted our names on at holidays. It has become a family treasure with some relatives dying, or leaving through divorce, and children and in-laws being added. There are twelve of us in our immediate family.

Like I said in the note I wrote to you when you were dying in New York, "The Tevises are populating southeast Ohio." Your name will be remembered long after we are both gone.

I talked with your sister Betty recently. She said, "I miss my brother."

I asked Will why you didn't leave us sooner. He answered, "He loved us. We were a family." A family is stronger than anything I can think of. In one of your letters you said, "We had some rough times but sometimes we were good together." We produced some wonderful children. Will and Julie can't be beat and are my best friends.

Going over the materials to write this book has given me some perspective on our relationship and peace to my soul. Why was I attracted to a person whose life and background were so different from my own is a question I have wrestled with all my life. Now I see that it could have been no other way. It was in the script. You were Fast Eddie Felson and Jerome Newton. You needed a warm-hearted, stable woman at the time I met you. We were in the same place at the same time. As your mother so generously once said, "If you hadn't married Jamie, you would have burned out your life long ago."

You were on your third, rural high school teaching job when I met you. Will came along early in our marriage. With a family to support, you realized you had to get on with your life — returning to graduate schools and later to a steady job as editor in the highway department. I doubt *The Hustler* would have been written if you had not had to keep office hours — writing while you waited for the research reports to come in to be edited.

In a relatively short time, you went from being a straggly

English teacher with a temporary teaching certificate to a writer of short stories and a book that has become a classic. Later, I helped you maintain your position in the community as a Professor, kept a home, and helped rear two children. On other domestic duties and responsibilities you were lax. You loved your children and liked having a family, but you were never able to be fully committed to us. I will have to admit that with my enabling, you were able to continue drinking.

This arrangement worked for many years. You and I shared one common goal — the parenting of our children. The children became more independent, and I took a teaching position. Our needs changed.

As you recovered from your alcoholism, your creativity began to return, and another woman appeared on the scene to help you with your writing and to attain your lifelong goal of living the New York lifestyle. You lived this life for six short years. For an undisciplined man, who never planned his life from one day to another, you did pretty well for yourself.

I recently overheard Will ask Julie if she thought their dad was a bad person. "He drank too much. He was lazy, sometimes didn't tell the truth, was not always a faithful husband."

Her answer was that he was a good person. "He never meant to hurt anyone although he caused a lot of pain. He loved us and was proud of our accomplishments. He was his own worst enemy."

You wrote about winners and losers. Here is an epitaph for a winner:

WALTER STONE TEVIS, Jr.
Born Feb. 28, 1928 – Died Aug. 9, 1984
A Son and Brother
Husband and Father
A Teacher, Author, Friend
He lived–He loved

Your Kentucky Wife,
Jamie

PART TWO:
THE WRITER

Jamie Tevis

INTRODUCTION

With Walter's epitaph, I finished the story of my life with the hustler. Now I can share some items that mostly are not a direct part of my life, but which may be of interest to Walter's fans. These are things that I know about Walter the writer that will be very hard to find elsewhere.

There are sections in this part on Walter the poet and Walter the letter-writing sailor. Those sections are followed by some scholarly reflections on Walter's work (with my comments and corrections!).

Part Two ends with a reprint of an interview with Walter from the *Courier-Journal* (Lexington, Kentucky) in 1980. I chose to end this part of the book about Walter the writer with this interview because it is full of direct quotes from him. I wanted to give him the last word.

WALTER THE POET

Walter's earliest writings are poems. Five short poems are preserved in a little book made by Walter for his parents. He probably wrote it before he even started school. The little book was so valued by his mother that it is one of the few objects that made the trip to Kentucky when the family moved from California during the Depression. She gave it to me soon after we married along with his little quilt and some toys. I made Walter a "this-is-your-life" scrapbook for his birthday one year, and the little book of poetry was included. The scrapbook is now in a trunk with Walter's papers that he left behind when he went to New York.

There were other early signs of special talent. "He was always articulate," his sister remembers. Pouring out a stream of words or silently immersed in a book, he showed early signs of verbal facility. Walter told me,"In the second grade, I was the one the principal sent for to read to the visiting lady from the Board of Education."

In college, Walter lived in a dank cellar, grew a beard, and wrote sonnets. While researching this book I came across a scrapbook with page eight from the March 1949 issue of the *Review of Contemporary Poetry*. It was a poem titled "On Metaphysics: With a Traitor." It was a short poem with several classical references. It ended this way:

"What is truth?" said Socrates.
"Truth," I said, and smiled smugly,
"Is correspondence undefiled."

When we first met, Walter showed me some poems to old girlfriends. I don't suppose it is an accident they got lost.

In his later adult life Walter only produced a handful of poems—two for me, one for Julie, and one for our friend Madelyn Kavanaugh. They have never been published. When Walter died, I gathered up his papers and magazines containing his stories and gave them to the University of Kentucky Library for safe keeping. I was not aware at the time that his will stated that all his literary works were to be left to Eleanora, his second wife.

While browsing on the Web, I came across a poem to myself, one to Julie he wrote her on her wedding day, and a list of the items I had given to the University of Kentucky Library. With some searching, I found out that all of the items I had donated to the Library were released to Eleanora. She sold them to the Lilly Library in Indiana. I was not able to get permission to use the copyrighted materials in this book. I am relying on the "fair use" law and my memory for the following section.

Jamie Tevis

WALTER THE LETTER-WRITING SAILOR

Walter's discharge papers show that he served for eleven months—from April 1945 until March 27, 1946.

Walter joined the Navy when he turned 17, advancing his age a year in order to enlist. He was only a junior in high school at the time. He said he wanted to see the world as World War II was coming to a close. It was more than that: it allowed him to get away from home and to prove to himself, his mother, and especially his father that he was an able-bodied young man.

Walter's mother saved at least a dozen letters he wrote during the Navy service. His sister Betty passed them on to me. They are also stored at the Lilly Library.

He always addressed the letters "Dear Folks," and they were read by his close-knit family. At the time his mother and father lived in Richmond, Kentucky. His older sister Betty Jean (B.J.) was attending the University of Kentucky. His letters were certainly shared with his Aunt Myra and Aunt Sallie, both living in Lexington.

Walter's Navy experience influenced his life in many ways, most of them positive. A very important thing that helped him to become a writer was the money that he got for college tuition from the G.I. bill. From the letters and from stories I heard through the years, I was able to piece together other ways that the seventeen-year-old boy's Navy service influenced the man.

Most of Walter's letters were scrawled on one sheet of paper. There is little indication they are written by the hand of a would-be fiction writer. In an early letter he wrote to his family from San Francisco, "Now that we are leaving the good old United States we are beginning to feel homesick. The glamour of being a sailor is wearing off. We are just a bunch of

Navy buddies.
Walter, Hilary Knight, and friend.

dumb kids, fresh out of boot camp, who are beginning to realize how unseaworthy we are."

For three months the ship sat in the rocky harbor of
Okinawa, and here were a number of short letters from there.
Walter described Okinawa as a bunch of big rocks jutting out
of the water. Since little was required of the men (a two-hour
watch every third day), there was lots of time to play cards,
eat, sleep, and do a little laundry. Jeans were washed by tying
them with a rope and dragging them behind the ship when it
was moving.

If the ship's calendar said it was the day to paint the deck,
the sailors were ordered to paint even if the water was rough
and washed it off as fast as it was applied. If it was the day to
scrape the sides of the ship, men were lowered down on rope
ladders and scraped even if it was storming. If they were ordered to wash the deck on a calm day, the method was to dash
it with buckets of water and then mop it. This is fine for a ship,
but if Walter was asked to mop our kitchen floor, he used the
same method. He wrote to the family that he was astonished
at the sloppy way the Navy is run. Walter had a tendency toward laziness and sloppy habits. I guess I can't blame the Navy
for that, but it didn't help.

He wrote that he was happy to have been assigned as a
ship's carpenter to a 900-man destroyer tender—a huge machine shop and repair station. He described the shop as a lazy
place. They worked two hours a day and then slacked off. In
spite of the slow pace, he learned carpentry, and Walter was
always proud of his carpentry skills. He used them to make
bookshelves, picture frames, coffee tables, and a cradle for Will.
Together, we went to antique and junk stores and found pieces
to repair and refinish for our home.

Walter was not a picky eater, but there were two things
he couldn't stand the sight of: fruit cocktail and Spam. One of
the men sawed into the storage area and brought out gallon
cans of fruit cocktail. Walter got sick from eating too much of

the syrupy fruit.

Toward the end of his year of service to his country he wrote, "I have at last found my liberty town, New Orleans. For the first few blocks there are nothing but barrooms and tattoo joints." He told his mother not to worry. He had not patronized either of them . . . "yet." He did, however, get drunk and his buddies had "Anne" in a heart tattooed on his hip, the name of a girl back home in his high school class. He was always proud of it and it grew as he grew in weight over the years.

He and his buddy, Hilary Knight, ate in "The Court of the Two Sisters" and in "Antoine's." They remained friends throughout his life. Hilary later illustrated the Eloise books about a precocious little girl who spent most of her time in the New York Plaza Hotel. Over the years, Walter visited him when he was in New York. Once Walter made a friend, he was always a friend.

Walter was discharged in San Francisco. At the time of his discharge, he was classified as Petty Officer third class — Yeoman. His photos from the time show a very tall, thin young man with his buddies. He had saved some money, and he hoped to visit Jenny, the family friend who had visited him in the hospital and who had put him on the train to join his family in Kentucky seven years earlier when he came home from the California Hospital. He was also looking forward to visiting places he had lived as a boy and to enjoying the city as he remembered it. While he was taking his last shower on the ship, someone stole his wallet. Once again, Jenny came to his rescue and made him a loan so that he could get home.

Walter's uniforms remained in a trunk for years. Not too long ago, I decided to give them to the local museum, but before doing so I took pictures of grandsons Jonathan and Caleb in Walter's Navy whites. With the legs rolled up, they were a good fit. The insignia on the arm (an eagle over crossed pens over a single stripe) is very clear on the sleeve. Caleb, with his cap tilted towards the side of his head, was seventeen when I took the photo—the same age Walter was when he joined the Navy. Walter's hair was blond and curly. Caleb's hair is blond but straight. Jonathan's hair is curly but deep brown. Walter would have been proud of his grandsons.

Granddad's navy uniform is a pretty good fit.

WALTER'S IMPACT AS A WRITER

In this section I have collected essays written about Walter and his work and sprinkled my own comments around them.

There are three essays by Kacey Kowars, whom I came to know when he was researching a book about Walter. Mr. Kowars did a lot of research for the project, but his life took a different direction, and he turned his papers over to me. I have extracted some very interesting insights he wrote. In the first essay, Mr. Kowars compares the life of Fast Eddie to Walter.

"Fast Eddie Felson"

Fast Eddie Felson

by Kacey Kowars

Fast Eddie Felson was an amalgamation of several of Walter Tevis' short story characters. The seven short stories that Tevis wrote all had a common set of characters. There was the wily veteran hustler, who evolved into the character of Minnesota Fats. This character was always heavyset, always an expert gambler, and always won the critical matches where a lot of money was on the line. The other principal character was the young hotshot who was out to knock the fat man off his throne. This character lived by his wits, and always ends up getting hustled himself. This character became Fast Eddie Felson.

Tevis told us little of Fast Eddie's background. We know he came from Oakland, California, and that his father owned an electronic-repair shop. Eddie tells us that his father spoke of only two things: the war he had fought in, and what he would do when he came into some money. We are given the impression that Eddie's father was a 'loser' in his son's eyes.

Fast Eddie's father bears a striking similarity to Walter Tevis' father. Tevis' father was a remote man who had difficulty communicating with his son. He was an alcoholic when Walter was a young boy. When the Tevis family moved back to Kentucky in 1939, Walter was left behind at the Stanford Children's Home. Tevis became emotionally moved when he discussed this period of his life. "I was left alone for about a year before I rejoined my family. San Francisco became my lost paradise." This notion of a lost paradise was used in *The Man Who Fell to Earth*.

"I write about losers and loners—if there's a common theme in my work, that's it," Tevis wrote. "I invented the phrase 'born loser' in *The Hustler*. In one way or another I'm obsessed with the struggle between winning and losing."

This part of Fast Eddie's personality, the "born loser," begins to surface in the final passages and stages of his classic battle with Minnesota Fats. Eddie has Fats on the ropes. Fats calls for a break. He goes into the bathroom and composes himself. He washes his face and hands, combs his hair, and straightens his tie. While Fats is grooming himself, Eddie drinks straight from the whiskey bottle. The match resumes. "Somewhere in Eddie, deep in him, a weight was being lifted away. And, deeper still, there was a tiny, distant voice, a thin anguished cry that said to him, sighing (You don't have to win). For hours there had been the weight, pressing on him, trying to break him and now these words, their fine and deep and true revelation, had come and were taking the weight from him. The weight of responsibility. And the small steel knife of fear."

Eddie proceeds to get drunk, losing his entire bankroll to Fats. By the end of the match, Eddie is broke. He is alone, a pathetic figure passed out in his own vomit on the poolroom floor.

This scene from the novel would return to haunt Walter Tevis, for in writing this classic battle of wills between Fast Eddie and Fats, he was foreshadowing the events that would come to pass in his own life. Tevis the writer was Felson the pool player. Coming from an obscure background Tevis wrote a first novel that was well-received and turned into a successful movie. He needed only to continue developing his craft and his

Jamie Tevis

dream of becoming an important American writer was within his grasp. His father never accepted Walter's decision to become a writer and a teacher. He felt that these two professions were 'feminine pursuits.'

In a letter to a friend, Tevis once wrote, "I made up Fast Eddie. Sarah might, in a way, be me; but that was in another country, and besides the wench is dead."

This last statement, Tevis as Sarah, is revealing. Tevis went through treatment for alcoholism in 1976. Thus, Walter Tevis was actually a blend of two of the characters in *The Hustler*. Fast Eddie was Tevis' idealized vision of himself. Eddie Felson was what Walter could never become. Eddie was bold, daring, well-coordinated, and cocky. He was the best pool player in the country. Sarah, meanwhile, was another part of Walter Tevis. She claimed to be a writer, but preferred drinking to writing. Tevis' alcoholism was transferred to the character of Sarah in the form of a limp. Tevis knew his drinking was a problem, as did Sarah. In the novel Fast Eddie is unable to make a commitment to Sarah. A part of him wants to, but pulls back at the last minute. In the movie Sarah commits suicide after sleeping with Bert Gordon. Not so in the novel. The novel rightly shows the reader that Fast Eddie and Sarah both want the same thing, but are too afraid to take the risk of failing; just as Walter Tevis could not merge the two sides of his personality, the creative writer and the man who wanted to prove his mother wrong, prove that he really was just like all the other boys, that he could be successful.

Walter Tevis would throw his talent away. Like Fast Eddie, Tevis would be unable to deal with the success of his early work. Bert's confrontation forces Eddie to take a serious look at his life. The beating he suffered at the hands of Minnesota Fats had shaken his confidence. And for a hustler, confidence is everything. Eddie drifts from bar to bar trying to hustle up a game, but instead finds himself drinking again.

Fast Eddie Felson is an extremely likable person as was Walter. He strikes up friendship rapidly wherever he goes; he has original and creative ways of looking at life and a genuine sense of vocation about his daily work. But his daily work is that of "hustler" or pool shark. He makes his living by preying on unwary pool players.

What Fast Eddie wants more than anything else in the world is to beat Minnesota Fats, the reigning top pool player, and to become kingpin himself. This seems to him to be the best possible good for himself. But, of course, this would be taken for evil by Minnesota Fats.

Reading this essay caused me to compare Walter's father and Fast Eddie's father. Both fathers lived for a time in Oakland, California, and had difficulty communicating with their sons. Eddie thought of his father as a loser. Walter's father had been crippled by the effects of the Depression. His father looked on Walter as a loser. Walter mentioned in an interview that telling your father you were going to be a writer was like saying, "I am a homosexual." Harry, his therapist, told Walter he had trouble topping his father. Perhaps Walter wrote about losers and winners because of his father's attitude toward him. He wanted to prove to his father that he was not a loser.

Mr. Kowars says Walter's character is revealed in Sara's limp, her physical flaw. Walter's drinking was his physical flaw, although he would not have admitted it at the time he wrote *The Hustler*. It seems a case of foreshadowing, a fear that his drinking was a flaw he did not allow to come to the surface. Before we were married I went to the house where he was rooming in Carlisle. There was a note stuck in the dresser mirror with a date written on it. I asked him what it meant, and he said he wanted to see how many days he could go without a drink. His books are filled with references to alcohol. An AA member once said his books were like a drunkard's diary. Later he spoke of the pain of addictive drinking, "It is not the physical pain like a burning ulcer, but the deception and the lying to self."

Mr. Kowars is correct in saying that Walter could never merge the two sides of his personality — the good boy his mother wanted him to be and the grown-up, strong-willed, mature man his father would have approved of. Eddie was the man Walter wanted to be.

At the end of his essay, Mr. Kowars notes that Eddie wanted more than anything else in the world to win at pool. I believe that Walter wanted more than anything to show his father he was worthy of his approval. I watched for years as Walter achieved great success. In the academic world, Walter attained the rank of Full Professor at Ohio University. He was nominated by students as University Professor of the year. He is in the University of Kentucky Hall of Distinguished Alumni. His books have been published in several languages and his movies viewed in many lands. He made lots of money. He produced children, and his grandchildren will carry on the family name. Yet Walter never got what he wanted most — his father's approval.

Walter was the Hustler — or more accurately, Walter became the Hustler. Over and over I've found complex ways that Walter was writing a blueprint for his own life when he wrote *The Hustler*. Eddie wanted to hustle pool above all else in his life. In the end, Walter wanted to write above all other desires in his life. Both of them left behind the people in their lives who had meant the most to them and took the big gamble that they could be successful at what they wanted to do most. Eddie left Sarah and Charlie, and Walter left his wife and children. The fate of Eddie's game was determined by Bert. The success of Walter's later writing and the management of his money were given over to his friend and second wife, Eleanora.

In the following piece, Mr. Kowars comments on the significant social impact of *The Hustler*.

"*The Hustler* and Pool Playing in America"

The Hustler and Pool Playing in America

by Kacey Kowars

Some 450 colleges installed an average of ten tables each. The recent popularity of bowling also helped. It had become perhaps the fastest-growing participant sport in the Fifties, and now many of the old bowling establishments were moving out of the basement into large, air-conditioned spaces, and the proprietors began putting in billiard centers as an added attraction. The new billiards centers also took on a new look. They were bright and cheerful and inviting, and they appealed to a new clientele. Women took up the game in record numbers, and it was not unusual to see whole families gathered around a pool table.

Brunswick, the world's largest manufacturer of pool tables, responded to the game's new look by sprucing up their equipment a bit. After some discussion, they replaced the traditional cloth with colors like beige, blue, gold, and tangerine. The tables also were remodeled and streamlined. They were outfitted with rotating numerals built into the frame of the table as a score-keeping mechanism, replacing the old button score markers strung on overhead wires that had to be flicked from one side to the other with the end of the cue stick. The whole package seemed to fit well together, because by the middle of 1962 orders for new tables were coming in so fast that Brunswick fell six months behind in filling them.

Paul Newman and Walter Tevis were the instigators of this initial resurgence in the game's popularity. They would repeat the trick again in 1987, with the re-

lease of the film *The Color of Money*.
Newman received an Oscar for his rec-
reation of the role of an older Fast Eddie
Felson in *The Color of Money*. The pool
halls would fill up again with young
men imitating Tom Cruise. Newman and
Tevis would both be voted into the Billiards Congress Hall of Fame, the only
two non-players to receive this honor.

Walter and I grew up before television. Walter was one
of the first to explore the long-range influence of this inven-
tion. In the next piece, Mr. Kowars compares Walter's opin-
ions about television with those of Neil Postman, author of
*Amusing Ourselves to Death: Public Discourse in the Age of Show
Business*.

"Early Analyists of Television: Walter Tevis and Neil Postman"

**Early Analysts of Television: Walter
Tevis and Neil Postman**

by Kacey Kowars

Walter Tevis would have agreed with
Mr. Postman. Tevis' work focused
heavily on the effect of television on
modern society. He first offered his criti-
cism of television in his second novel,
The Man Who Fell to Earth, written in
1960, published in 1963. Thomas
Jerome Newton, the alien in the novel,

studies American culture by watching
our television shows in outer space.

Newton visits an attorney named
Farnsworth after landing on Earth from
the planet Anthea. Newton makes the
following observation of Farnsworth's
bedroom: "His room was high-ceilinged
and ornately furnished. He noticed a
television set built into the wall in such
a way that it could be viewed from his
bed and he smiled tiredly on seeing it—
he would have to watch it sometime, to
see how their reception compared with
that on Anthea. And it would be amusing to see some of the shows again. He
had always liked the Westerns, even
though the quiz programs and the Sunday 'educational' shows had provided
his staff at home with most of the information that he had memorized. He had
not seen a television show for a long
time as the trip took four months."

As the novel progresses Newton is far
too busy opening and developing busi-
nesses to pay attention to television. But
his success becomes tiresome and he
discovers the seductive allure of alcohol. He begins to drink; moderately at
first, only wine. Then he progresses to
gin, and his drinking increases. As he
falls into alcoholism he begins watching
television again, in the solitary confine
of his bedroom.

Newton knows that his cover has been
blown, that the FBI is on to him. Newton is listening to music one evening,

when he decides to turn on his television: "Then he walked to the television controls and turned them on—maybe a Western . . ." Tevis wrote this passage in 1960—long before the advent of cable television and satellite dishes— but he saw the ultimate outcome of offering people multiple-viewing options. Decades before the term "channel-surfer" was first coined, Tevis's character, Thomas Jerome Newton, had become a channel-surfer.

In 1960 television, and the country was falling in love with John F. Kennedy and with Camelot. Political discourse had moved from the age of typography into the age of show business. And, as Neil Postman says, "Therein is our problem, for television is at its most trivial and, therefore, most dangerous when its aspirations are high, when it presents itself as a carrier of important cultural conversations. "

Tevis saw what was happening with the advent of television, yet he himself could not turn his own television set off. He drank like an alcoholic for the next seventeen years. When he sobered up in 1976, he realized that he needed to make some very basic changes in his life, besides the obvious need to stop drinking. One change was to give up television. In a lecture he delivered to students at the University of Kentucky in 1982, he said: "YOU must purge TV from your heart, mind and soul. I find this very hard to do, myself, even though I watch little

TV. But it is, I think, absolutely necessary if you are going to locate your own
experience in any useful way."

When Tevis sobered up in 1976 he
found he had woken up in a society that
was losing its desire to read books. His
return to fiction, *Mockingbird*, published
in 1980, was originally titled *The Last
Man Who Could Read*. Tevis was concerned with the continued dominance
that television had assumed in people's
lives. He was also aware of an increasing level of infatuation with all things
technological.

The following material was prepared for Dr. William Ellis'
English class by Lisa English at Eastern University, Richmond,
Kentucky. The material is posted on the internet at KYLIT - a
site devoted to Kentucky Writers:
http://www.arh.eku.edu/ENG/services/kylit/tevis.htm

The following piece is about coincidental moments. The
author, Mike Zempter, and I happen to be in a writing group
at our library here in Athens, Ohio. When he heard my name,
he remembered that the book *The Man Who Fell to Earth* had
been dedicated to me. Mike wrote this essay for me to explain
how he had been affected when he read that one of the characters was from his own hometown, Portsmouth, Ohio.

This is for Jamie Tevis, in my writers'
group, former wife of Walter Tevis who
wrote *The Man Who Fell to Earth*.

- Mike Zempter April 7, 2001

"Remote Transmission Through Walter Tevis"

Remote Transmission Through Walter Tevis

by Mike Zempter

I went several thousand miles out from my home place to encounter Walter. I strayed from the Ohio commons into the Colorado heath, and there I sat my rocking chair and passed some time flying that craft, and one night there was a visitation.

I don't know why I picked up *The Man Who Fell to Earth*. Well, I know, yes, but I don't know why.

The thing of it was, and is, that I never much read any science fiction, not even as a boy. In all my life, I only ever made it through maybe half a dozen sci-fi novels. I just rarely picked them up, and when I did happen to select one out, it usually did very little for me, and within maybe 20 pages, I became an Invisible Man and slipped from the reading area.

It might have been the title. *The Man Who Fell to Earth* is, after all, a real title, the kind that stands on its own as an aspect of art. Rare, and profound. Think about it.

The Man Who Fell to Earth.

The Man Who Fell.

The Man Who.

Like the cry of an unknown bird. I felt

lucky to hear it once. It echoes in my
mind to this day. I followed it along the
tree line at the twilight's last gleaming. I
think it flew off into my mind, because
it long since immediately became a part
of my thought. Part of the atmosphere of
my life. A man falling. The looks he
might have on his face. The background
he came falling out of. The foreground
he came falling into. The Man Who Fell.

I saw him hit this earth, and laboriously
pick himself up, and dust himself off.
Lonely work. In a way I can say I
joined him there for company. He has
been a boon companion.

I met him one night out there, in my
rocking chair, in a suburb of Denver.
Something alerted me—the rush of
wind—so that I sat rocking, mesmer-
ized, as my spirit went off into that
book.

It was the story of the first alien, who
was a profoundly alienated man. Who
made passage to this rock out of dire
emergency, and crash-landed, and set
about his forlorn mission, helped along
by this human discovery named alcohol.

He was a lonely man, and walked a
ragged mile here, at this inhospitable
site. But he found a little company for
himself, and he and one of his compan-
ions would go off together sometimes,
in the evening, to drink and consult the
same muse – whichever it is that lives in
the sky. They would drink themselves
drunk, and shoot the breeze, and say

goodnight again, and go off to their
beds.

The human friend that the alien made
was also alienated. Also alcoholic, it appeared. Each thought rather deeply on
the other. The human, it turned out, had
suspicions.

One night, on the shore of a lake, this
native to the earth felt his suspicion
reach critical mass, and asked of his odd
friend, in all seriousness – in fact, in
high seriousness –

"Are you from Mars?"

A long look, in silence. Then the man
who was being questioned answered, at
this high point in human history, hidden
out by a lake, in the night, under alcoholic haze, where nobody else could
hear:

"Of course I am." And they had that
conversation, well-realized.

At length, having come to know his
friend, the Martian asked, "Are you
from Mars?"

The man who had not fallen answered,
"Farther away than that. I'm from
Portsmouth, Ohio."

I will never forget this incident, this passage from this book, this passage
through a night of my own life, as long
as I live. Page 158.

I had been rocking, and then I stopped in
mid-arc, leaning over the book, trying to
come to terms with what I was seeing.
It could not be, and yet it was, and when

it had sunk into me, the shock was so
profound that I must have seized up and
recoiled in my rocker, because I tipped
the chair over backwards and fell out on
the floor, gripping the book.

It was as if a ghost had finally appeared,
after a life of blind faith. I had certainty,
and I went briskly to the phone and
called all the way back where I had
come from, back home, and then I read
about five pages to a loved one, finishing with that passage above.

I heard her stammer and ask of me the
same questions my mind had just asked
the voice that does not answer aloud,
and I laughed, not so much from the humor of it, because it wasn't a piece of
humor. I laughed with the pleasure of
the thing. The ultimate surprise and
deepening suspicion that there was an
answer, and not only had I known it, all
along, but finally I held it in my hand.

Her reaction was still at the level of dis-
belief, or denial, when we got off the
phone, and I stood alone again by my
overturned chair, looking down at the
words, and out at the night.

You see, I myself came from a place
called Portsmouth, Ohio. And I won-

dered why he had chosen us, or why we had been chosen, and especially a few of us. And I wondered all through the years, until the wondering had become part of who I am.

The Man Who Fell to Earth. And the man who stood there waiting for him— Walter Tevis. In the movie he was David Bowie. In another sense, in a way that still matters, he was me.

INTERVIEW WITH WALTER

The following article is from *The Courier-Journal Maga-zine*, Saturday. January, 27, 1980. It is reprinted here with permission of the copyright holder, the Courier-Journal & Louisville Times Co.

"Toasting the Best of Times"

Toasting the Best of Times: Former Kentuckian Walter Tevis quaffs the heady liquor of literary success

by Shirley Williams

His years of drinking were the worst of times for Walter Tevis, a writer who spent his formative years in Lexington, Ky.

For 17 years he did not publish a book.

Now it is the best of times for Tevis, who will be 52 next month. He has been "on the wagon" for nearly five years. His third novel, *Mockingbird* (Doubleday. 247 pp. $10), published this month, garnered a small fortune for him *before* publication through the sales of paperback and foreign rights. It is a science-fiction novel, set in America in the 26th century.

Yet to come are royalties from the hardcover sales of *Mockingbird* and, inevitably, a movie. (As early as last November, according to Tevis, three movie companies and actor Dustin Hoffman were looking over his manuscript.)

"With the help of my psychotherapist, who is a real jim-dandy psychotherapist, and some other things that are going for me, I am happier than I have ever been in my life," Tevis, who now lives in New York City, said in Louisville recently. "And," he added, "I'm healthier. You should have seen me when I was drinking. I've got pictures of myself taken 10 years ago in which I look older than I do now."

Tevis has published only two previous novels, but they both became modern classics and were made into movies. *The Hustler*, Tevis' first novel, was about a poolroom hustler and became a film starring Paul Newman and Jackie Gleason. The film version of his second novel, a science-fiction piece called *The Man Who Fell to Earth*, starred British rock star David Bowie, and the paperback edition of the book starred Bowie on the cover.

"I tried to convince Avon Books that putting him on the cover might be a mistake," said a chuckling Tevis, "because Bowie fans aren't likely to be people who read books in the first place. But," he added reflectively, "he's a very fine man. I liked him a lot. Thank God. Because on the American edition of the book, which came out with the movie, David Bowie's name on the cover is about twice as big as mine, and it looks like he wrote it. If I had hated his guts it would have been terribly hard to take."

The Bowie film was not nearly as successful in America as *The Hustler*, due, Tevis said, to poor distribution, but it did well in Europe. "I was at the premiere in New York and there were an awful lot of slack-jawed 15- and 16-year-olds. They had come expecting him to sing. So maybe the word got around with Bowie fans. It [the movie] sure didn't help sell the book. "*The Hustler* was published in 1959," Tevis continued. "The movie came out in '61. Then I grabbed the money that I made from the movie and went to live in Mexico with my family and discovered that you could get gin for 80 cents a liter. I stayed drunk for eight months, then sobered up and wrote *The Man Who Fell to Earth*. All the good people in *The Man Who*

Fell to Earth drink. My man from Mars becomes a hopeless alcoholic."

Could Tevis write when he was drinking?

"No. I never could combine the two. One drink and the typewriter was completely out of the question. I never work continuously on a book. I still work only in spurts. I'm very fast. I write a short story at a sitting. I wrote the first third of *The Hustler* in one week and a three-day weekend. All my stuff up until *Mockingbird* had been corrected rough draft. When I go to write, the words come to me very easily, and the stories, the ideas. Everything is just wonderful, and I don't have any trouble with it at all. It's just that I can't seem to make it work more than one day out of 15 or so."

Much of his fiction is almost unalloyed autobiography, using experiences that go back nearly 40 years. He was born in San Francisco. When he was 10, his father went broke. "It was the tail end of the Depression," he said. "We are from an old Kentucky family, the first family, I think, to hold a deed in Madison County. My father had been born in Kentucky, and he came back to live with his sister. He was without a job and without money."

Because of a rheumatic heart, Tevis was left behind by his family in a San Francisco hospital. "I was in California for about a year when they were gone," he said. "They really shut me off." He put this experience to use in *The Man Who Fell to Earth.*

"The main idea in the book was, you know, here's this guy who comes from another planet and he's tall and skinny, which I was. I was incredibly thin and tall for my age. He can't walk very well. Everything seems heavy to him and there's this tremendous culture shock. And that was a way of dealing with the way I felt when I first came here [to Kentucky].

"I came here and was traumatized by my entrance into the Ashland School in Lexington at the age of 11. That's so painful I don't think I can talk about it."

But he found that he could.

"My accent was strange, I was nearly crippled from having a rheumatic heart and rheumatic fever. That's what *The Man Who Fell to Earth* is all about. He can't take the gravity on earth and lands in Kentucky, in Estill County. I used Estill County because I taught school there and I liked the sound of the name.

"The fact is that most of the themes from my writing I learned in Kentucky. I learned to shoot pool in Lexington at the Phoenix Hotel poolroom. And I learned to read science fiction here. Oh, boy. I have a hard time being loquacious about it. I've got some uncomfortable feelings. It was a very bad few years.

"I was physically weak. I got beat up a

lot by the kids in school. I just really could hardly handle it. It's something I'm going through in psychoanalysis right now and have been for some time. And it is especially traumatic because I am doing an autobiographical novel, some of which takes place in Lexington.

"Anyway I got acclimated, and by the time I was at the University of Kentucky I liked it a lot. I was in A.B. Guthrie Jr.'s writing class."

Tevis' first published work, a short story, was in *Esquire*. "It was about a pool hustler," he said. "It was written in Bud Guthrie's graduate creative writing class and was called 'The Best in the Country.' I've published 13 short stories about pool players in various national magazines and then I published the novel. I stole the title for *The Hustler* from a story I had published in *Playboy*, also called 'The Hustler,' but not really resembling the novel."

He also tried to write about the five years he spent teaching high school in Kentucky. "I started a novel and got about 100 pages of it, and sometime I would like to finish it," Tevis said. He also worked for the Kentucky Highway Department for about a year, during which he wrote many short stories.

Also, Tevis continued, "I postponed, I think, the development of the malady [alcoholism] by teaching in dry counties for five years. All the way through, one characteristic of my alcoholic drinking was that I would never build up a supply. If they weren't selling liquor on Sundays I didn't drink on Sundays. I would go to a friend's house and bum a drink, but I would not buy a bottle on Saturday night to pass me through Sunday.

"I didn't have a car—I didn't learn how to drive until I was in my 30s—I just couldn't drink in those places except sometimes when I would hitch-hike to Lexington and get drunk.

"I really don't know whether I could answer the question of whether I liked living here or not," he continued. "It's like–on Tuesdays and Thursdays in New York, when I'm asked where I'm from, I say Kentucky. On Wednesdays and Fridays I say California."

What does he say on Saturdays and Sundays?

"Ohio."

Tevis was relaxed and affable during the interview. He looks like a slightly rumpled bed; it is impossible to imagine him with every hair in place, a tie precisely knotted, a handkerchief in his breast pocket. He asked for a drink, then laughingly explained that he wanted "club soda, Perrier water, or anything like that."

He is no longer thin. Lifting weights every other day at a health club in New York keeps his tall, wiry frame in shape, and, he claims, is the current secret of his writing success. He walks a lot, has learned to cook, and is threatening to join the Manhattan Chess Club. His biggest problem these days is the desire to be more productive.

"I haven't had a cold in a year and a half," he boasted. "I eat everything I want and I lose weight. I do a lot of things just to occupy the time between days when I am able to write. I sit in front of the typewriter every morning. And I *can* force it. But when I force it it's just no damn good."

He qualified that a little.

"It's good, but it's not good enough to suit me. I could make an OK hack writer. Sometimes I think I should write dumb novels under an assumed name just to give me something to do."

Tevis feels he became an alcoholic because he couldn't handle success, couldn't handle topping his father.

"I went to Mexico to write *The Man Who Fell to Earth*. You know the continuing story. I got drunk and stayed that way until I was 47. My therapist says that I couldn't compete with my father, I couldn't surpass my father. He would never accept me as a writer. He considered being a writer—announcing for a writer—was like announcing you were a homosexual. And so he died on me just before I published *The Hustler*."

His mother was a source of problems, too. "I was brought up by a very castrating mother," Tevis said, "the kind who absolutely made me keep my nose clean and my fingernails clean and wouldn't let me play with the other boys on the block because they were nasty—that kind of thing. The Lexington poolrooms rescued me. I learned to swear in the poolrooms.

"I blame my alcoholism on a lot of things. One of the most interesting ones is that when I was in the convalescent hospital I was kept quiet by being given three shot glasses full of Phenobarbital a day with every meal. They gave it to all us kids. They didn't have tranquilizers in those days. They kept us silent in bed. We were supposed to sleep most of the time; we weren't allowed to talk during meals.

"Phenobarbital is a more addictive substance than alcohol. I don't know what the dosage was. I tried to find that out. I was at that hospital three weeks ago in California for the first time since 1939. My voice trembles to speak of it."

Through the years of drinking Tevis managed to teach, though he didn't manage to write. He now is on leave from the English department of Ohio University at Athens, Ohio, and doubts that he will go back. "I'm a full professor of English, and I was able to do that and do it well," he said. "I was never drunk in class or anything like that. I just drank from like midnight till four in the morning and got up and taught my classes."

His crisp voice takes on a tinge of sadness as he talks about the lost years and the changes he had to make to come to terms with sobriety.

"I felt it necessary to change my life utterly in all kinds of ways. I'm an alcoholic and it began with my stopping drinking quite a few years ago. I put myself into an alcoholic ward at a hospital. I wasn't drunk at the time. I hadn't had a drink in 10 months, but I felt I needed it or I would be drinking again.

"I don't know that I was addicted to it, but I took a lot of Librium for a year or so, never in increasing doses; I just took three pills a day. When I put myself in the alcoholic ward they shocked me by taking my Librium away from me. I went through the DTs [delirium tremens] from Librium withdrawal. The treatment center I went to did not give you anything except a muscle relaxant for the first three days lest you go into alcoholic withdrawal–DT's–and kill yourself. DTs is a much more fatal disease than most people realize."

His praise for the treatment center is wholehearted. "It was a terrific place, a fine enlightened, humane place, you know. This was in Columbus, Ohio, at St. Anthony's Hospital. Just a damned good place. And I learned a lot of very hard truths about myself and I got sober and, thank God, I stayed sober. In the last speech from the director of the hos-

pital, he told us, 'When you go home,
don't try to quit smoking, don't quit
your job, don't divorce your wife. Don't
do anything like that for a year. Just act
like a sick dog and crawl under the
porch and heal.'

"I felt he was right, that I shouldn't
make any major decisions in my life for
a year. Just not drink. Stay cool. So I did
that and I stayed cool for another year,
and then I began to realize that I just had
to start changing things. I was starting to
count the days until retirement with my
job. And I had a good pleasant job and a
good salary. I felt I just had to change
everything.

"It wasn't as mechanical as that," he
continued thoughtfully. "I didn't say,
'Well, let's check off the things; let me
see now. Well, I've got to change my li-
cense plates, divorce my wife, stop the
milk'–it wasn't like that. The marriage
had a lot of terrible tensions in it. And I
still care for her a lot, I really do, and
it's heartbreaking in a lot of ways. But it
seemed absolutely necessary, just to
break all the ties. The marriage had gone
to hell, anyway. A marriage in which
one member is an alcoholic is a mess
and some of the messes that I created
will always be there." Tevis has two
children from the marriage, a son, 26,
and a daughter, 22. Both are married.

Another thing that changed his life,
Tevis said, was "all of that middle-aged
crisis that I went through. The kids leav-

ing home and getting married. I think it
began when I was promoted to a full
professor.

"I was elected to what they call university professor—a pretty high honor—
and made full professor and all that
stuff. And I discovered along the way
that I was far more ambitious than I had
ever let on to myself. Other people had
seen it, but I hadn't spotted it in me.
When I got to the top of the place I was
at work, I realized, Jesus, I'm not interested. Also I realized after I had finished
my 25th year in teaching—that's too
much! I don't need to do it anymore.
You know. I was beginning to repeat my
jokes."

His divorce was final a year and a half
ago, and that's when he moved to New
York. The woman in his life now is from
Scotland, Eleanora Walker, to whom
Mockingbird is dedicated. "She spots
the bull in my writing," Tevis said,
laughing. "She's good at it.

"Even though my productivity is up, I
still write very little on a working day.
About five or six weeks ago I got going
for one week and I wrote three long
short stories in one week, and they are
all very good, and I've already sold two
of them.

"I just go crazy. I don't have any of the
conventional props. I don't have a wife.
I don't have children. I don't have a job.
and I don't even have a house, other
than the apartment. I can't putter

251

around. If anything needs fixing you call the super and it gets fixed.

"I've got New York City at my disposal. If I'm bored, I've got no excuse for being bored. I all at once find myself with about 73 excuses for not working and for not enjoying my life. It is incumbent on me not only to work but to be happy. It's a terrible struggle, but I feel great, sure do. I'd just like to be more productive. I'd like to work two or three hours a day. That's all I really need. I'm an expert at puttering around.

"I felt very guilty about the money I made out of *The Hustler*, and I thought I had violated my artistic integrity to get all that kind of money. Now I'm delighted. I used to go around apologizing to everybody for making money out of my stories and books."

Tevis has been working on an autobiographical novel; its working title is "Drunk." He finished about 300 manuscript pages, then put it aside. "I haven't yet decided whether to do a totally new novel or to finish the autobiographical one," he explained. "There's reason to wait for more distance. It includes as one of its major portions the effect on me of moving to New York, which I only did a year and a half ago. It's all pretty close material.

"Most of my stories have been disguised autobiography. I just felt it was time I did one that wasn't much disguised. The autobiographical novel is about myself as an alcoholic. It's the most painful thing, it was a real horror show for about eight or 10 years. It's that way for every drunk, too, it's just that way. Some drunks really have a death wish and really do themselves in. I sometimes think that I did it as long as I could get away with it. It's a horrible way to go.

"I'm not thinking about physical problems like cirrhosis, but the psychological pain, the pain of keeping the pain a secret from yourself and things like that. The fears are overwhelming. This is not just me. I know a lot of people very well in AA [Alcoholics Anonymous]. I'm a very strong AA member right now.

"The organization protects itself. It doesn't want any of us reformed drunks being spokesmen for AA. That's a very wise policy. There's a lot of honesty in AA, but there's also a good deal of simplification and it feels like a Rotary Club sometimes. It's like Sunday School. . . . A lot of these people are regressing to youthful notions of decency that are associated with the church, with the guilt they have accumulated.

"Well, good, serious, hard-core alcoholics are gentle and charming people, and male alcoholics are very good at exploiting women; something I am trying to write about, too. They try to make women into their mothers and they want to be taken care of. I want to expose the whole racket if I have the courage. I can't expose the whole general racket, which is maybe something I try to do too much, but to expose my own rackets. The ones that I've pulled."

After shelving his autobiographical manuscript, Tevis "took up doing a collection of short stories; six old science-fiction stories written about 20-odd years ago," he said, "all of them written in Kentucky, by the way, most of them when I was working for the Kentucky Highway Department. I decided to put them together with six new ones. The book's gonna be called *Far From Home* and is divided in two halves. The first half is called 'Far From Home' and the second half 'Close to Home.'

"I intend to write an introduction to explain that by 'Far From Home' I mean a kind of old-fashioned science fiction that doesn't touch anything meaningful in the life very closely, that is essentially a bunch of cerebral ideas, cute tricks, what-if stories, gimmick stories, which a lot of science fiction is. Anyway, I make use of my chess-playing mentality. I'm a very good chess player and the stories make ideas click along kinda neatly and come out neatly at the end.

"The second half of the book is something that is very important to me, the most important thing in my work in a long, long time. It is what I consider to be a new kind of science fiction; it's used almost entirely for a kind of psychoanalytic myth-making. It's about my Oedipus complex and my narcissism and a lot of things of that sort.

"I feel the stories are very good. I feel that they are some of the best things I have ever written. They are close to home in that they are meant to deal with the feelings that I find in myself most powerfully and most affecting and most unresolved. There is a tremendous sophomoric quality to most science fiction, and yet I love it. I've been hooked on it ever since I read *The Wizard of Oz*. I'm crazy about the themes, and I'm crazy about the subject matter, but there has been so little grown-up stuff written. I've been trying to be the grown-up science-fiction writer ever since I wrote *The Man Who Fell to Earth* [in 1961].

"I don't believe in inventing brand new plots. I would like them given to me and then concern myself with what I really want to do when I write, which is finding out what I have to say in the act of saying it. And what I've done in my late stories is to go further in the direction of using science fiction as a vehicle for a psychological story. I'm very pleased with what I've been writing. More excited in many ways about my book of stories coming out [probably in the spring] than I am about *Mockingbird*.

"My lifetime can be predicted by what I write. I may be clairvoyant. In *The Hustler*, Eddie ruins his pool game and success by getting drunk. And the man who fell to earth becomes a hopeless alcoholic. And *Mockingbird*, which I actu-

ally started before I left Ohio, has an
Ohio professor going to New York, and
at the end of the book he takes his
woman and is going to California, and
I'm planning to do that, too. And I'm not
doing it because I wrote it in the book.
There are an enormous number of little
incidents. I have no willingness to accept any kind of supernatural claims
whatever, but there are all sorts of things
that have worked out that way.

"When I was getting suicidal in Ohio
many years ago and developing a fantasy—I developed a lot of fantasies—I
was living in New York and living on
the top of a building with big French
doors overlooking the skyline and writing a novel. And sonuvabitch if I don't
have big French doors in this apartment
and I didn't even know they were there
when I rented it. And you can see the
Hotel Pierre right outside the window
and I'm on the top of the building in the
penthouse. It was the only apartment I
could find."

Tevis expects to be back in Kentucky as
he develops his "Drunk" manuscript. He
is revisiting the scenes of his earlier life.
(His sister, Ms. Betty Tevis, lives in
Lexington and is employed by the University of Kentucky.) Coming here last
November for the celebration of Kentucky Writing at the University of Louisville was one of the first steps, three
weeks after a backward look at California.

"I flew first-class to San Francisco and back, and they were pouring champagne all through the flight both ways," Tevis said. "I feel as though my spiritual growth is complete, that I sat there and drank orange juice. That's why I consider myself a saint and not a mere angel.

"Anything else you want to know about me? I can't think. I'm happy, I'm working, I'd like to be able to work every day."

Jamie Tevis

Jamie Tevis

A WALTER TEVIS BIBLIOGRAPHY

Novels:

The Hustler. New York, Harper & Brothers, 1959.

The Man Who Fell to Earth. New York, Gold Medal Books, 1963.

Mockingbird. New York, Doubleday, 1980.

Far From Home. New York, Doubleday, 1981.

Steps of the Sun. New York, Doubleday, 1983.

The Queen's Gambit. New York, Random House, 1983.

The Color of Money. New York, Warner books, 1984.

Short Stories (in order of date of publication):

"The Best in the Country." *Esquire*. November, 1954.

"The Big Hustle." *Collier's Magazine*. August 5, 1955.

"Misleading Lady." *The American Magazine*. October, 1955.

"Mother of the Artist." *Everywoman's*. 1955.

"The Man from Chicago." *Bluebook*. January, 1956.

"The Stubbornest Man." *The Saturday Evening Post*. January 19, 1957, *John Bull*. (London). June 29, 1957, *Familie Journal*. (Copenhagen). September, 1957.

"The Hustler." (original title, "The Actors") *Playboy*. 1953

"Operation Gold Brick." *If*. June, 1957.

"The Big Bounce." *Galaxy*. February, 1958.

"Sucker's Game." *Redbook*. August, 1958.

"First Love." *Redbook.* August, 1958.

"Far From Home." *The Magazine of Fantasy and Science Fiction.* December, 1958.

"Alien Love." (Author's title: "The Man from Budapest") *Cosmopolitan.* January, 1959.

"A Short Ride in the Dark." *The Toronto Star Weekly* Magazine. April 4, 1959.

"Gentle is the Gunman." *The Saturday Evening Post.* August 13, 1960.

"Farnsworth's Eye." *Galaxy.* 1960.

"The Other End of the Line." *The Magazine of Fantasy and Science Fiction.* 1961.

"The Machine that Hustled Pool." *Nugget.* February, 1961.

" Machine Record." *Science Fiction Adventures* (London). Vol. 4, No. 20, 1961.

"The Scholar's Disciple." *College English.* October, 1969.

"The King is Dead." *Playboy.* September, 1973.

Magazine Articles:
"A Key to Magazine Fiction." *Writer's Digest.* August, 1959.
"The New Rooms." *The Nation.* 1965.
"Input Your Move." *The Courier Journal.* Sunday, May 29, 1974.

"Checkmate in Vegas." *The Atlantic Monthly*. October, 1974.

"Fastest Man with a Cue." *Sports Illustrated*. December 16, 1974.

Unpublished Stories :

"Cobweb." (circa 1951)

"Turnip Island." (circa 1980)

Poetry:

Untitled poetry collection. Manuscript in Jamie Tevis' private collection, (circa 1932).

"On Metaphysics: With a Traitor." *Review of Contemporary Poetry*, Vol. 1, March 1949, Lexington, Kentucky.

"Jamie After Sixteen Years." Manuscript in the Lilly Library, Indiana University, 1968.

"A Poem: for Madelyn, Who Moves Fast." The Lilly Library, Indiana University, October 16, 1972.

"December Twenty-Second, Nineteen Seventy-Three." The Lilly Library, Indiana University, 1973.

"To Julie in Her White Dress." The Lilly Library, Indiana University, 1979.

Letters:

Letters written from the Navy, collection of letters in the Lilly Library, Indiana University, (1945-1946).

SOURCES

Kowars, Kacey. "Fast Eddie Felson." Previously unpublished essay.

Kowars, Kacey. "*The Hustler* and Pool Playing in America." Previously unpublished essay.

Kowars, Kacey. "Early Analysts of Television: Walter Tevis and Neil Postman." Previously unpublished essay.

Mosconi,Willie and Stanley Cohen. *Willie's Game*. Macmillen, 1993. pp 217&218.

Dr. William Ellis and the English Department of Eastern Kentucky University with Lisa English. Bibliography, 1984.

Williams, Shirley. "Toasting the Best of Times." *The Courier-Journal Magazine*. January 27, 1980. pp 8-13.

Tevis, Jamie. "My Life with the Hustler." *The Kentucky Review*. Vol X Number 3. University of Kentucky Press.

Echdahl, Betty Tevis FKA Betty Tevis Balke (sister of Walter Tevis). "Pool Player Turned Into the Hustler." *Richmond Register*, 1967.

Dan Nather. "Remembering Walter Tevis." *The Athens News*. Athens, Ohio. September 27, 1984.

Time, January 12, 1959.
New York Times, January 25, 1959.
Neikirk, William. "Look Back at Irvine's 'Ichabod'." *Chicago Tribune*, August 1984.
Donald Richter. "Chess with Walter." Written 2001 for inclusion in this book.

Warren, Jim. *Herald-Leader*. Lexington, Kentucky.

Jamie Tevis

Neil Postman, *Amusing Ourselves to Death: Public Discourse in the Age of Show Business.*

University of Kentucky Alumni Hall of Fame
The Lilly Library <Liblilly@indiana.edu>
Unpublished stories, manuscripts and papers.

Other Sources:

Toby Kavanaugh, August 27, 1984. Personal correspondence.

Frank and Florence Mathias, 1984. Personal correspondence.

Paul Newman, Feb. 6, 2002. Personal correspondence.

Clarence Page, Nov. 5, 2001. Personal correspondence.

Tuan Van Pham, Dec. 24, 2001. Personal correspondence.

Reid Sinclair. "Conversations with Walter," 2002. Written specifically for this book.

Mike Zempter "Remote Transmission Through Walter Tevis," 2001. Personal communication.